CLIMBERS AND
WALL PLANTS

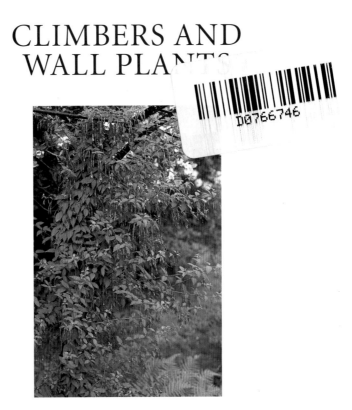

CLIMBERS AND WALL PLANTS

A PRACTICAL GUIDE

Sue Spielberg

THE NATIONAL TRUST

Published in Great Britain in 1998
The National Trust (Enterprises) Ltd
36 Queen Anne's Gate
London SW1H 9AS

ISBN 0 7078 0214 8

Cataloguing in Publication Data is available from the
British Library

All photographs come from the National Trust Photographic
Library and are by the following photographers:
Stephen Robson: front cover, half-title page, 6, 8, 9, 10, 11, 12,
14, 15, 16, back cover
Neil Campbell-Sharp: frontispiece, 13

Line drawings by Jim Robins

Designed and Typeset in Palatino by the
Newton Engert Partnership

Printed in Great Britain by Butler & Tanner Limited

HALF TITLE: In bloom from mid-summer until the end of
autumn, *Fuchsia* 'Riccartonii' provides unbeatable flower
power for the hooped metal archway at Penrhyn.

FRONTISPIECE: Large-flowered clematis such as the candy-
pink 'Nelly Moser' provide interest at eye level on the brick
and timber pergola at Barrington Court, while the apricot-
white shrub rose 'Penelope' dominates the foreground.

Contents

Introduction

At first glance, climbers, wall shrubs and wall-trained fruit trees seem to have little in common, but what unites them is their ability to clothe the vertical plane. As such they should be cherished for being among the most indispensable and versatile plants for the garden: without them it would be harder to soften the hard lines of buildings, disguise less-than-beautiful fences, camouflage eyesores or decorate arches, pergolas, walkways and trellis screens. The smaller the garden, the more potent the argument for employing their services, for compared with their ultimate size, they take up very little ground space. As anyone who gardens in a plot the size of a pocket handkerchief will explain, when it comes to maximising its potential, the only way is up.

The sky really is the limit when it comes to choosing the plants for such 'vertical gardening', and who better to turn to for advice than the Head Gardeners of the National Trust who grow them? *Climbers and Wall Plants* is the second title in a series tackling specific gardening topics, which has come about in response to our desire to tap into the Trust's deep reservoir of expertise. I am indebted to all who generously gave up their time to help me compile the information in this book.

Although I could have chosen from countless others, the ten gardens that form the backbone of this book were selected to give as broad a range as possible. Westbury Court and Felbrigg Hall are well known for their wall-trained fruit trees, while much of the charm of other productive gardens like Barrington Court and Erddig lies in their arresting displays of ornamental wall shrubs and climbers. Gardens from different geographical locations have been chosen to highlight how climate governs planting. From Sizergh Castle in the north of England to Cotehele in the south-west, from Penrhyn Castle on the north-west coast of Wales to Blickling Hall near the north coast of Norfolk – all illustrate the importance of exploiting favourable microclimates within the garden to extend the range of plants that can be grown with success.

The Head Gardeners may hold contradictory opinions on pruning and general maintenance, but all agree on the importance of tailoring the plant to suit the spot and not the other way about. With this in mind, the final section of the book is devoted to the plants themselves, enabling you to make an informed choice. Whether you are developing a new garden or looking to improve an existing one, there is a rich repository of plants capable of fulfilling your dreams. The great thing is to experiment – like the gardeners of the National Trust – to see what works for you in your own garden.

The striking red autumn tints of Boston ivy, *Parthenocissus tricuspidata*, soften rather than totally conceal the ancient stone walls of the pele tower at Sizergh Castle.

A luxuriant combination of
Clematis 'Perle d' Azur',
euphorbia, agapanthus and
achillea at Powis.

Powis

I am quite sure that if Violet, Countess of Powis and wife of the
4th Earl, who donated the property to the Trust in 1952, were
alive today, she would not be disappointed with the garden
she helped to embellish during the early twentieth century.
Many would say that her ambition to turn 'a poor and meagre
garden' into 'one of the most beautiful, if not the most beautiful, in England and Wales' has been admirably achieved with
some of the credit going to her and the rest to the National
Trust's gardeners.

Perched on a hill overlooking a large tract of countryside
towards the Severn valley, the fortified castle was built by
Welsh princes in the thirteenth century to keep out the
marauding English. Although the early history of the garden
is sketchy, the terraces are thought to have been designed for
William Herbert, 1st Marquess of Powis, by the architect
William Winde towards the end of the seventeenth century.
In 1705, an impressive water garden in the Dutch style was
added on the flatter terrain now known as the Great Lawn,

but this was dismantled in 1809. The next important phase came after 1912 when Violet, Countess of Powis, replaced the kitchen garden to the east of the terraces with the present formal gardens.

Powis has continued to evolve and develop under the care of the National Trust. The most significant change has been to the planting arrangements, which today are recognised as among the finest in Britain, thanks in part to former Head Gardener Jimmy Hancock, who worked at Powis for twenty-five years, and did much to focus attention on tender perennials for summer use in borders and containers.

Blickling

With its leaded windows, curving Dutch gables and corner turrets, Blickling Hall is an enchanting building that is not easily forgotten, especially if the onlooker is fortunate enough to see its mellow, terracotta-coloured brickwork bathed in the evening sunlight.

The present house was built by a rich lawyer, Sir Henry Hobart, in 1619, and over the last three hundred years his descendants have left their successive marks on the gardens, each adding their own contribution in line with the fashion of the day. Although now vanished, the original design laid out for Sir Henry would have been formal, featuring a number of enclosures as well as a dovehouse and mount. The garden depicted in 1729 on a survey plan commissioned by the 1st Earl of Buckinghamshire, was again largely formal – a rectangular garden to the east of the house, with geometric planting designs and a great terrace walk at the far end. But by the end of the eighteenth century, the 2nd Earl had altered the formal avenues into the park and created a network of meandering paths within it, under the influence of the contemporary English Landscape Movement.

The evolution of the gardens came full circle when a number of the 1st Earl's formal schemes were revived in the late nineteenth century. An elaborate parterre of beds was laid out on the lawns of the east front, and the whole area was enclosed by a buttressed brick retaining wall, complete with flights of steps and bays for seats. So it remained until the 1930s, when Norah Lindsay was engaged to simplify the scheme, and what visitors enjoy today is the result of this remodelling. Gone is the multiplicity of dotted beds; the area is now graced by four large square borders filled with blocks of subtly graded colour. The two nearest the house are given over to pink, blue, mauve and white, while a yellow and orange theme is the order of the day in the pair beyond.

Lonicera periclymenum and *Geranium* 'Johnson's Blue' at Blickling Hall.

Cotehele

Nestled at the top of a steep wooded valley that opens out onto the west bank of the River Tamar lies the granite, slate and sandstone house of Cotehele, with its gables and towers. The building dates back to the fifteenth century, and for nearly six hundred years, until the estate passed to the National Trust, it was owned by the Edgcumbe family, who enriched the house and developed the garden, which now extends to about 5·7 hectares (14 acres).

Although traces of a much earlier age still survive in the garden in the form of a medieval stewpond and a domed dovecote, the present design largely dates back to Victorian times. The formal layouts surrounding the house and the informal Valley Garden were both enhanced in the early nineteenth century, and many new plants were introduced by the 3rd Earl of Mount Edgcumbe at this time.

Even at Cotehele in the mild south-west of Britain, *Clianthus puniceus* requires the shelter of a warm, south-facing wall to ensure it produces its striking claw-like flowers from spring to early summer.

A billowing froth of colour in the Rose Garden at Nymans in June. The vertical metal supports almost disappear beneath a veil of pale pink 'Adélaïde d' Orléans', shell-pink 'Debutante' and white 'Thalia'; soft pink 'Fantin-Latour' and darker pink 'Comte de Chambord' make up the shrub rose planting in the foreground.

Nymans

It is easy to run out of superlatives when trying to describe the garden at Nymans. Even the most fastidious visitor could not fail to be impressed by the spring-flowering narcissi and snake's head fritillaries that stud the grass beneath large magnolias; the strident twin summer borders filled with a profusion of colourful annuals and perennials; the swooningly fragrant froth of roses throughout June and July; not to mention the rare collection of trees and shrubs introduced from around the world by a number of eminent plant-collectors. In fact, that somewhat elusive notion of year-round interest seems particularly pertinent to this garden in the Sussex Weald, so much so that a number of return visits are required to really do it justice.

The garden at Nymans is the result of three generations of the Messel family. First came German-born stockbroker Ludwig Messel, who laid out the framework and introduced rare and hybrid rhododendrons from 1890 to 1915. He was succeeded by his eldest son, Leonard Messel, who together with his wife Maud, built the pastiche fourteenth-century manor house and added more exotics and old roses. In turn their daughter, Anne Rosse, played a significant part in continuing to enrich and improve the plantings after the property was given to the National Trust in 1953.

Penrhyn

Like the rugged peaks of the landscape it overlooks to the south, Penrhyn Castle is similarly stark and imposing. Sandwiched between the Menai Strait and Snowdonia, the huge, pale grey, neo-Norman castle was constructed between 1820 and 1845 by Thomas Hopper for George Hay Dawkins Pennant. Why Hopper and Pennant chose such an austere style for a family home remains a mystery, though one member of the family recalled, 'Mr Hopper used to come in after breakfast and ask leave to add another tower'.

In keeping with the scale and importance of the new building, the grounds were redeveloped and enlarged. This process coincided with the age of the great plant-hunting expeditions, led by such intrepid explorers as David Douglas and Robert Fortune, whose introductions were snapped up with all the voracity of chocoholics at a sweet shop. Many of the new tree and shrub species inevitably found their way to Penrhyn.

It also marked the beginning of the influence of Walter Speed, who reigned supreme as Head Gardener for fifty-eight years, starting around 1860. A leading expert on fruit and

Influenced by the Gulf Stream, the mild climate at Penrhyn Castle in North Wales favours the use of tender plants such as fuchsias. Here they clothe a long arched walkway that runs the width of the Walled Garden to provide an intimate tunnel dripping with flowers.

flower production, he put Penrhyn on the map as a centre for horticultural excellence. His Walled Garden on the west side of the hilly site enjoyed all the benefits of the Gulf Stream, enabling him and his successors to grow tender plants like the present spectacular arches of *Fuchsia* 'Riccartonii'.

Sizergh

Rising from the rugged Cumbrian landscape, Sizergh Castle, home of the Strickland family for over 750 years, can be seen for miles around. Although it looks rather imposing when viewed from afar, its stark edifice, which is shrouded in a veil of Boston ivy, gives no hint of the intimate 6·5-hectare (16-acre) garden that lies at its foot. The jewel in the crown of the Sizergh estate is the rock garden which was constructed from typical Lakeland stone in 1926 by a local firm, Hayes of Ambleside. Covering about an acre, it boasts winding walks, splashing streams and a string of rock pools, around which are planted alpines, moisture-loving perennials, dwarf conifers and Japanese maples. It is also home to part of the National Collection of hardy ferns.

Barrington

Set in gently rolling countryside just off the Somerset Levels, the garden at Barrington Court possesses a certain detached, almost dream-like tranquillity. Perhaps because it does not lie on a highly publicised, well-beaten tourist track, or maybe because it is still run along traditional lines, with its walled enclosures and bountiful kitchen garden, it is a bit like tripping over a time warp and stepping back to the hazy, lazy days of the 1920s and 1930s.

Although Barrington Court was donated to the Trust in 1907, the restoration of the Tudor house and creation of the 4·5-hectare (11-acre) park and garden were largely down to the Lyle family who took over the tenancy in 1920. It was in these early years that Colonel Lyle commissioned the architects Forbes and Tate to carry out work on the old house, convert the seventeenth-century Strode stable block into a house, and build the subsidiary estate buildings. Forbes also came up with designs for the garden, and the elderly Gertrude Jekyll, who was by then in her seventies, was invited to draw up plans and planting schemes for parts of it. Today Barrington Court is the best example of her work within the National Trust's care. Interestingly, she never actually visited the garden in person: all the information she required was sent to her, including soil samples packaged up in biscuit tins!

Individual colours are preferred over mixed shades for the sweet pea wigwams in the walled kitchen garden at Barrington Court.

The south-facing brick walls and well-drained soil at Felbrigg Hall are ideal for more tender shrubs like *Ceanothus* 'Southmead', which produces its rich blue flowers from late spring to early summer.

Felbrigg

As the crow flies, Felbrigg Hall is about a mile away from the North Sea, but its protective belt of parkland, made up of venerable old beech, oak and sweet chestnut trees, affords a certain degree of shelter to an otherwise inhospitable location. A curious fusion of both early and late seventeenth-century architecture, the Hall is set within formal grounds, but it is the magnificent old walled garden a short distance from the mansion that is the real *pièce de résistance* at Felbrigg.

Covering approximately 1 hectare (2·75 acres), the walled garden is now primarily ornamental, but allusions to its past as a highly productive kitchen garden, providing enough fresh fruit and vegetables for the resident family and their domestic staff, have been cleverly retained. Orderly rows of vegetables may have given way to luxuriant drifts of herbaceous perennials, but the wall-trained fruit trees of bygone times are still very much in evidence. Likewise, the handsome eighteenth-century dovecote, probably designed by the architect James Paine while he was working on the service wing of the main house, and a pair of large lean-to glasshouses not only make valuable focal points in the enclosure, but serve as constant reminders of the garden's more utilitarian past.

With their spring blossom and autumn fruit, the espaliered apples at Westbury Court provide two seasons of interest.

Westbury

Westbury is a very fortunate garden indeed, for it came within a hair's breadth of being destroyed forever. Had not fate looked upon it so kindly back in the 1960s, Britain might have lost one of its rarest types of garden. The natural landscaping zeal of Capability Brown, Humphry Repton and their eighteenth-century contemporaries had elsewhere all but swept away the formal layouts of earlier times, but Westbury Court is yet more remarkable, for it is one of the finest examples of a late seventeenth-century Dutch-style garden. Not even in Holland has a garden of this kind survived to the same extent.

The garden was largely the creation of a local Gloucestershire gentleman, Maynard Colchester, laid out between 1696 and 1705. Quite why he chose this style remains a mystery. Possibly he was influenced by his close friend and neighbour, Catherine Boevey, the daughter of an Amsterdam merchant. Whatever the reason, the garden was small in scale, divided by long, rectangular canals, enclosed by hedges and topiary specimens and boasted many kinds of ornamental shrubs and bulbs, as well as more productive fruit trees and vegetables, making it far more Dutch than French in character.

Alterations and additions to the garden were made by his

Clematis 'Jackmanii' and the pink rambler rose 'Dorothy Perkins' festoon a series of wooden posts at Erddig. Careful pruning is required to prevent one overwhelming the other.

nephew and successor, Maynard Colchester II, between 1715 and 1748, but thereafter the history of Westbury Court is one of neglect and decay. In 1960 it was sold to a speculator who demolished the nineteenth-century house and the long west wall, and was about to fill in the canals when Gloucestershire County Council and the Rural District Council stepped in to buy the land in 1964. A home for the elderly was built on the area north-west of the present drive, but the main part of the garden was offered to the National Trust. Spiralling costs meant the Trust was unable to accept the property until 1967, when enough money was secured to pay for its restoration and upkeep.

Erddig

As so often happens with gardens down the centuries, original layouts are greatly altered or simply swept away in accordance with the fashions of the age. Fortunately for visitors today, this was not the case at Erddig, near Wrexham, whose late seventeenth-century formal framework is still very much in evidence. The property was given to the National Trust by Philip Yorke, whose ancestor, Simon Yorke, inherited the property from his uncle in 1733. Admittedly, succeeding generations of Yorkes have left their mark on the estate over the years – for example the park was landscaped between 1766 and 1782, and small formal parterres were added in both Victorian and Edwardian times – but the original pattern of the walled garden was never destroyed.

By the 1970s, this enclosed area was languishing beneath a thicket of brambles, nettles, long grass and overgrown trees and hedges. Philip Yorke cleared the central vista in the garden, introducing several sheep and a goat – which he referred to as his gardeners – to crop the grass. When the National Trust took over in 1973, an engraved bird's-eye view of the estate, drawn in 1739 by Thomas Badeslade, not only showed how little the essential elements of the garden had changed, it also formed the basis of their restoration. Today the bones of the garden, complete with broad axial walks, canal, hedges, lawns and orchards, so typical of the Dutch style of William and Mary, have been revived and reconstructed, while later plantings and additions made by the Yorke family are also preserved where they do not conflict with the original layout.

Powis Castle

Area: 10ha (25 acres)
Soil: acid woodland area, otherwise neutral to alkaline/clay
Altitude: 0–137m (0–450ft)
Average rainfall: 813mm (32in)
Average winter climate: cold

Undeniably, Jimmy Hancock, Head Gardener at Powis from 1970 to 1996, is a tough act to follow, but present Head Gardener Peter Hall is already proving himself a worthy successor. His long and varied career with the National Trust began as an assistant gardener at Wimpole Hall, Cambridgeshire, in 1978. Since then he has been in charge at Canons Ashby in Northamptonshire, Dunham Massey in Cheshire, and Stourhead Landscape Garden in Wiltshire, before finally succumbing to the lure of Powis in 1996. 'This is a garden I had admired for a long time. With its combination of history, its variety of plants and the opportunities to further develop the planting, it had everything as far as I was concerned,' says Peter in his quietly spoken, carefully considered way.

What of the future? Although Peter does not see huge changes to the planting at Powis, he has identified aspects which could prolong the displays. 'The garden tends to peak between July and September, therefore I would like to work on providing further interest for the spring and autumn,' he explains. Also in the past there has been a tendency to over-use tender and unusual climbers simply to exploit the micro-climates. Although Peter hopes to continue this practice, he will not dismiss using hardy plants where they work well. And if he can link the planting to historical traditions, then so much the better. 'In future I would like to have an eye open to the past. For example, peaches and other tender fruit would have been traditionally grown on the warm terraces at Powis. I cannot envisage a total return to that practice, but would be happy to experiment with more ornamental fan-trained fruit,' he admits.

Climbers and wall plants at Powis

The four Italianate terraces, which spill down the precipitous slope immediately below the imposing, pinkish façade of the castle, boast several natural advantages. Firstly, they face south-east and are therefore protected from the prevailing winds. Secondly, the heavy, limy soil has received so much organic matter over the years that it has reached that blissful state of being rich and moisture-retentive but also having good drainage. Thirdly, the high brick walls trap the sun's heat, not least in winter to provide sheltered warmth for a number of tender shrubs and climbers, like the flame-red *Abutilon* 'Patrick Synge', lemon *Lapageria* 'Yellow Trumpet', clear pink *Mutisia ilicifolia* and buttercup-yellow *Fremontodendron californicum*. 'It is amazing how much difference the walls make,' says Assistant Head Gardener Mick Evans. 'At Sissinghurst Garden in Kent, where I used to work, we admittedly enjoyed longer, hotter summers than here at Powis, but we rarely managed to overwinter the tender plants outside because the winters were so much colder.'

Further down away from the terraces tender plants give way to hardier subjects. Climbing roses and clematis along with remnants of gnarled, vertical cordon pears festoon the wall alongside the Croquet Lawn, while pillar roses and honeysuckles provide a vertical accent in the adjacent formal garden. 'Over the years the planting style at Powis has become lush and natural while still within a rigid framework. Although it is relaxed and can look almost unmanaged, it is never allowed to get completely out of control. Climbers and wall shrubs are important in softening the hard landscape, a fine blending of horticulture with architecture,' says Peter.

How to choose climbers and wall plants

The criteria for selecting the most appropriate climbing plants for a given situation are very much the same whether you garden on a grand scale on a hill in Powys or simply want to brighten up a handkerchief-sized plot in the middle of London or Manchester. Bear these important points in mind when making your choice:

● Will it complement the colour and foliage combinations of the existing plants in the immediate area?

For example, most gardeners would agree that a strident pink rose planted next to golden hop will not do either plant any favours. But replace the rose with the velvety purple-blue *Clematis* 'Jackmanii Superba' and visual harmony is once more restored.

● Will the climber complement its background?

This is less of a problem when dealing with natural stone or brick that has mellowed over time, but a modern red brick wall may clash violently with some flowers, such as the pink and white-striped *Clematis* 'Nelly Moser', and autumn foliage like Boston ivy, or *Parthenocissus tricuspidata*.

● What special effects do you want to achieve with the climber?

Ivy, for instance, will provide an evergreen cloak to soften a building or screen an eyesore, but deciduous Virginia creeper will only offer cover for six months of the year.

● Which plants will thrive, rather than merely survive, in the given site?

Familiarity with the aspect, soil type and the quirks of your garden, such as frost pockets or windy spots, will not only allow you to take advantage of any favourable microclimates, but it will also help you choose the right plant for notoriously difficult areas. For example, garrya, ivy and winter jasmine are surprisingly good on a north-facing wall, while pyracantha, parthenocissus and *Euonymus fortunei* cope well with city pollution as well as cold, windy sites.

● Select the plant carefully to suit the site, and always consider its ultimate height and spread.

Clematis at Powis

Many varieties of clematis are tucked in around the garden at Powis. With their scrambling habit, they are not always particularly elegant plants in themselves – until they flower, that is – but grow them upwards through more rigid shrubs and trees, and suddenly they are at home. This is hardly surprising, for in the wild these sociable climbers are never more content than with their feet in shade, their heads in sun and their long arms draped over the shoulders of woody neighbours.

Jimmy Hancock used their natural lolling tendency to great effect at Powis. 'He liked to see plants growing in their own way, which is why he did not restrict them unless he had to,' recalls Mick. On the Orangery Terrace, the purple-leaved vine, *Vitis vinifera* 'Purpurea', a double, dark red climbing rose, and deep blue *Clematis* 'Lord Nevill' is just one example of a *ménage à trois* happily sharing the same bed because all are similarly vigorous.

The famous wrought iron 'Jackman hoops', which consist of eight arches joined at the top, are an important feature either side of the path at the west end of the Orangery Terrace. Originally supports for the rich purple *Clematis* 'Jackmanii Superba', from which they presumably took their name, they are now home to a wider variety of spring- and summer-flowering clematis, adding height to the borders without obscuring the plants around them.

How to prune clematis

Clematis basically fall into one of three pruning groups:

Group 1

These flower early in the year on the previous season's ripened wood. Examples include *C. alpina*, *C. cirrhosa*, *C. macropetala* and *C. montana*.

● Prune immediately after flowering, removing dead or damaged stems and reducing others to keep them within their allotted space.

Pruning clematis from group 1.

● To renovate a neglected specimen, cut back all stems to healthy shoots near the base immediately after flowering. Feed and water well, and do not repeat the pruning process for at least three years.

Group 2
These are all large-flowered hybrids and flower in early summer on the previous season's ripened wood and then again in late summer on new growth. Examples include C. 'Nelly Moser', 'The President', 'Henryi', 'Lasurstern', 'Marie Boisselot' and 'Bees' Jubilee'.

● Remove dead and damaged stems in early spring, and prune all remaining ones back to where strong buds are visible on the main framework.

● To rejuvenate overgrown specimens, Mick recommends cutting back half the plant to the base to initiate bud break below ground level. If it responds well, do the same with the remaining half the following year.

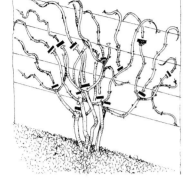

Pruning clematis from group 2.

Group 3
These flower in late summer on new growth made in that season. Examples include C. *viticella*, C. *texensis*, C. *orientalis*, C. *tangutica* and some large-flowered hybrids, such as C. 'Comtesse de Bouchaud', 'Hagley Hybrid', 'Jackmanii Superba', 'Perle d'Azur' and 'Rouge Cardinal', that bloom in late summer.

● Prune in late winter or early spring, cutting back to strong pairs of buds about 15–30 cm (6–12 in) above ground level.

If you are still in any doubt as to their pruning, Peter advises tackling clematis after they have flowered, so you not only benefit from the blooms, but also give the plant a whole season to recover.

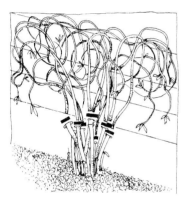

Pruning clematis from group 3.

General cultivation tips for clematis
● Plant clematis with the top of the rootball at least 8 cm (3 in) below the soil. This will encourage new growth to come up from stem buds below ground level if clematis wilt strikes the aerial portion of the plant. Keep their roots cool in summer with a thick mulch of garden compost or well-rotted manure applied in late winter, or even a flagstone placed over the soil.

● At Powis clematis are tied in at least once a week. It would be far too laborious to tie in each individual stem, so five or six shoots are loosely bundled together and fastened with soft garden twine. 'Initially this looks a bit unnatural, but after a few days you really wouldn't know it had been done,' admits Mick.

Layering clematis.

● You do not necessarily have to dig up and replant a clematis if you planted it in the wrong place. Providing the distance is not excessive, dig a trench in the appropriate direction, lay the stem along it, ensuring that the growing tip is still visible, and refirm with soil. This is particularly suitable where a dense network of roots is unfavourable for establishing clematis – for instance round the base of a tree or large shrub.

Planting climbers and wall plants

Peter prefers to plant hardy climbers in autumn rather than spring. Not only is the soil naturally warmer after the summer, but rain is more or less assured at this time of year, so encouraging the establishment of a healthy root system. He believes in preparing a generous planting hole and breaking up large clods of earth, but he does not automatically incorporate organic matter, unless the soil is especially poor or dry. 'I feel the plant should be encouraged to spread out its roots into the surrounding soil as soon as possible. If its immediate environment is too favourable, it may never send out roots to search for nutrients and water, and it will then suffer when conditions become drier,' he explains. He also warns against planting too close to a wall. 'The root system should be at least 15cm (6in) from the base to avoid the natural overhang and subsequent rain shadow.'

Ties and supports

Although strategically placed vine eyes will hold main branches in place, a system of parallel wires is the most convenient and aesthetically pleasing means of tying in the majority of climbers and wall shrubs. Four or five courses, about 30–45cm (12–18in) apart, is usually sufficient for most walls and fences. Carefully installed, the wires should last at least twenty years, so it is worth taking the initial time and effort to do a thorough job.

'It is important to tie the string tightly to the wire but loosely onto the plant to allow some room for growth,' says Peter. Natural products, such as soft string for green wood and tarred twine for woody branches, are best because they will eventually rot. Twist ties and wire are often forgotten, and as they never erode, they act like tourniquets, cutting into the bark and stopping the vital flow of food and water up and down the stems.

Renovating wall-trained climbing roses

Like clematis, climbing roses are very much a part of Powis. 'In the past Jimmy let them grow fairly naturally because he liked to see them flowering above great herbaceous swathes in the borders. Admittedly this looked great, but it also meant that for about two months early in the season there was a tide-mark effect on the walls, with nothing filling the gap between roses and emerging perennials. We are trying a new pruning style with them now, which will hopefully create a more even coverage of growth and flowers, but will still retain that relaxed look Jimmy used to strive for,' explains Mick.

Basically this involves carefully bending over and tying in the long stems to produce a framework of arching growth. Just as training climbers horizontally is often advocated to increase flowering, this hooping-over stimulates the growth of dormant buds near the bend so that new growth can be tied in lower down. 'In this way I am hoping to cut out all the oldest stems within three to five years but also cover a good proportion of the wall,' says Mick. 'It is very rewarding to bring an old plant round. Not only is vigorous growth more resistant to disease, it also produces more and better quality flowers in the long run,' adds Peter.

To renovate a neglected climbing rose without sacrificing the flowers, Mick recommends the following:

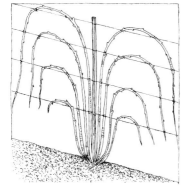

A wall-trained climbing rose pruned the Powis way.

● Prune any time between Christmas and early spring.

● Start by removing any dead, dying, diseased or damaged wood using a pruning saw or loppers.

● Cut out the oldest wood (approximately one-fifth to one-third of the main bulk of the rose) right down to ground level, or to the lowest strong shoot.

● Re-tie the remaining long stems evenly to cover the wall, arching them over to create a cascade effect.

● Vigorous laterals on the main stems can also be arched and reduced by a third of their length by making an angled cut just above a healthy bud or shoot. Smaller, weaker shoots should be cut back to two or three buds to initiate flower growth.

Pruning climbing roses on free-standing posts
In the formal garden near the timber-framed bothy, a series of free-standing larch posts, which support matching pairs of roses, line the main path and add height to the area. Although strapped to the post, the long stems are encouraged to arch over the top to produce a graceful, weeping effect. Golden *Rosa* 'Alister Stella Gray', apricot *R.* 'Alchymist' and yellowy-pink *R.* 'Phyllis Bide' all respond well to this style of training because they have a lax habit, but the growth of pink *R.* 'New Dawn' has proved far too stiff and angular to be effective.

To encourage flowering all the way up the stems, follow Mick's advice:

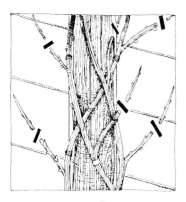

Pruning back the laterals of a post-trained climbing rose to four or five buds.

● Pruning can be carried out any time between Christmas and early spring, depending on the hardiness of the rose.

● Untie the entire plant and lay it out on the ground.

● Aim to cut out about one-fifth of the plant each year, cutting out the oldest, weakest stems first to encourage new growth for future years. Do not tip back any of the long, healthy, arching growth towards the top of the pole.

● Re-tie the climber to the post.

● If the rose is bare lower down, prune back any long, vigorous shoots arising near the base of the plant, to about half or two-thirds of their length, and twist them tightly around the post, tying them in securely as you go.

● To encourage flowers all the way up the column, prune back the laterals to about four or five buds; any more than that and you risk encouraging vigorous growth at the expense of flowering wood.

Pruning a vine pergola

With its underplanting of bright golden marjoram, the vine tunnel, reputedly on the site of the former grape house, makes an intriguing feature in the Formal Garden and helps break up the large expanse of lawn. Constructed from metal hoops to form a more or less continuous pergola across the grass, it is more ornamental than productive. Three types of vine, *Vitis vinifera*, *V.* 'Brant' and *V. coignetiae*, clothe the structure, providing dappled shade in summer followed by spectacular autumn colour later in the season.

If you have the space to accommodate them, vines are ideal for walkways and pergolas, and since they are vigorous, they hold particular appeal for the impatient gardener. If you grow *V. coignetiae*, Mick recommends keeping pruning to an absolute minimum. 'Surprisingly, the harder you cut it back, the more of a thug it becomes,' he laughs.

Contrary to all the textbooks that tell you vine pruning should only be carried out in winter to prevent sap bleeding from the wounds, Mick starts pruning the vines at Powis from May to June, as soon as the unfurling leaves are about the size of a postage stamp. The following regime is recommended where vines are cultivated more for their aesthetic appearance, rather than their fruiting potential, and especially where they do not benefit from the shelter of a wall:

● Cut back to a live bud all the dead growth on the wood made during the previous season.

● Two or three weeks later tie in the new growth to cover the supporting framework. Continue to do this on a regular basis.

● In early July, by which time the supporting structure will probably be covered with leafy growth, prune back the new stems to the point where the trusses of grapes are begining to form. This not only keeps the vine under control but it also allows more fruit to develop.

Tips

● Do not be in too much of a hurry to reach the top of the support when growing climbers and wall shrubs, unless you are content to finish up with a lollipop against the wall. Much more satisfactory results will be obtained if you encourage and tie in as horizontally as possible all lateral growth near the bottom of the plant first.

● Match the vigour of the plant with its intended situation. 'I have seen lots of mistakes made by people who choose the wrong plant in the first place.' For example, *Clematis montana*, which can scale dizzy heights of over 10m (33ft), looks about as comfortable as one of the Harlem Globetrotters in a Mini Metro when grown on the average boundary fence!

● If a climbing rose obstinately refuses to produce shoots from lower down despite your best efforts, disguise the bare area with a clematis or a shrub rose.

● It is worth investing the initial time and effort in erecting a decent framework of wires, to which plants can be tied. Do not resort to using netting – stems invariably grow through and behind it which can make the task of pruning a nightmare. This happened with the yellow Banksian rose, flanking the Orangery at Powis. 'No one had been brave enough to tackle it for about six years, even though it should be pruned every couple of seasons,' says Mick. It was only when its billowing mass began to encroach on the adjacent path that huge lumps were removed from its centre, but it was not a job that anyone relished.

Blickling Hall

NORFOLK

Area: 18·6 ha (46 acres)
Soil: acid/loam
Altitude: 30m (100ft)
Average rainfall: 580mm (23in)
Average winter climate: cold

The garden at Blickling is maintained by Owen Sayer and his staff of four. Visitors to the property may well become bewitched by it, but the place obviously holds an equally special appeal for Owen himself, considering he has been happily employed there for the last thirty-six years. Taken on by the Trust in 1961, he worked his way up and became Head Gardener in 1987. 'Although I look forward to coming to work every day, winter is my favourite time of year because that is when we carry out our restoration work. It gives us something different to do other than maintenance.'

Climbers and wall plants at Blickling Hall

Many of the wall shrubs and climbers grown at Blickling nestle in the dry moat, a reminder of an earlier house, drained some time before 1611. Shielded from the worst of the cold winds, this sunken garden, which now boasts a closely mown sward where the water once flowed, provides an ideal microclimate for plants that would otherwise fail in this part of the country. The red-stemmed evergreen *Rosa laevigata* 'Cooperi', or 'Cooper's Burmese' rose, normally considered tender, thrives here and freely produces its single, pink-tinged white flowers. Also flourishing nearby is the far from hardy *Trachelospermum jasminoides* 'Variegatum', with its white-splashed evergreen foliage and fragrant white flowers.

A mixed planting of shrubs and climbers means there is something of interest throughout the year. White *Viburnum plicatum tomentosum*, blue rosemary and pink *Buddleja farreri*, with its grey-white felted young stems and foliage vie for attention in spring. *Magnolia grandiflora* also starts to produce its long succession of ivory chalices. Mid-summer heralds the appearance of climbing roses such as yellow *R.* 'Golden Showers' and apricot *R.* 'Leverkusen', as well as the beautiful soft orange honeysuckle, *Lonicera* × *tellmanniana*. The visiting season closes with an autumn flourish of hardy fuchsias, pink and white *Abelia* × *grandiflora*, caryopteris, ceratostigma and *Hydrangea aspera* Villosa Group. None of the plants are allowed to grow any higher than the bottom of the ground-floor windows of the Hall because this would not be in keeping with a seventeenth-century house of this kind.

The retaining brick walls around the Parterre are host to a range of rambling and climbing roses. Cultivars include the butter-yellow *Rosa* 'Emily Gray', pale yellow 'Goldfinch', golden-yellow 'Maigold' and creamy white 'Silver Moon' on the north-facing wall, while the buff-coloured 'Gloire de Dijon', bright red 'Paul's Scarlet Climber' and apricot-pink 'Lady Waterlow' grace the west-facing wall. They share the border with herbaceous perennials, many of which grow so tall that they almost obscure the wall behind. To ensure the roses also get a look-in, Owen encourages them to grow vertically before fanning out their stems in either direction along the top of the wall.

Pruning guidelines

For many gardeners pruning is fuelled by fear: they have in their mind's eye an image of how a plant should look and the height to which it should grow, but once it has reached that point, mild panic sets in, out come the loppers, and the unfortunate specimen is often reduced to an ungainly shadow of its former self. True, most wall plants do need a certain amount of pruning to keep them to their allotted space, but this should not be your sole aim in brandishing the secateurs; maintaining a vigorous supply of healthy new shoots, and encouraging flowers and fruiting are equally valid reasons.

'Understanding the plant's natural habit of growth, and recognising whether it flowers on new or old wood, will help you prune wall shrubs and climbers,' says Owen. He classifies them into four main groups, and gives examples of those growing against the house and garden walls at Blickling:

● Those that flower between mid-summer and autumn normally do so on growth made in the current year. Pruning of these plants is best carried out in late winter or early spring so that the maximum time is available to develop the flowering wood. If left to their own devices they soon become a twiggy or tangled mass, producing smaller and fewer flowers. Cut back last year's growth to within one or two buds of the permanent framework (**a**). Examples of this are deciduous ceanothus, caryopteris and late-flowering clematis. *Vitis vinifera* cultivars also fit into this group, but should be pruned in mid-winter before the sap rises to prevent 'bleeding.' Prune back to within two buds of the main framework.

● Those that flower before mid-June on growth made the previous season. If you cut these back in winter or spring, you will be removing the flowering wood, therefore the best time to prune them is immediately after flowering. Cut back flowered stems to vigorous young shoots developing lower down on the main stems. Also remove to ground level about one-quarter of the oldest stems (**b**). Examples of this are *Buddleja farreri*, early-flowering clematis, *Lonicera* × *tellmanniana* and *L. tragophylla*.

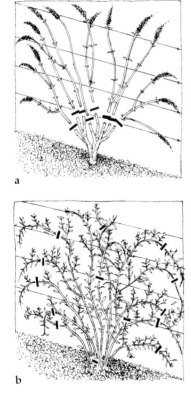

The main pruning methods for climbers and wall shrubs at Blickling include cutting back all the previous year's growth to a permanent framework (**a**) and removing flowered wood immediately after flowering (**b**).

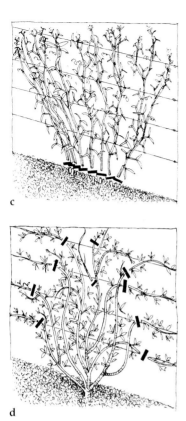

Cutting back herbaceous climbers in spring (**c**) and pruning to maintain the symmetry of the plant (**d**).

● Climbers which are more or less herbaceous and shoot from the base each spring. Cut back to ground level in February or March (**c**). Examples of this are the golden hop and perennial sweet pea, *Lathyrus latifolius*.

● Those which require only minimal pruning to keep them within bounds and maintain the overall symmetry of the plant. A portion of the oldest wood can be removed from time to time, cutting back to a vigorous replacement shoot lower down. Cut out any dead, damaged or diseased wood as soon as it is spotted (**d**). Examples include *Magnolia grandiflora*, trachelospermum, schizophragma, *Hydrangea anomala* subsp. *petiolaris* and evergreen ceanothus.

Wall shrubs and climbers for north- and east-facing walls

Located as it is on the flat, windswept plains of Norfolk, no more than ten miles from the North Sea, Blickling Hall has its share of climatic problems. Cold north and easterly winds, allied to an annual rainfall of just 58cm (23in), conspire to make it an inhospitable site for many plants. Even though the surrounding woodland does much to filter the wind, Owen still has to overcome many problems caused by it: whole limbs of wisteria and *Magnolia grandiflora* have been broken by blustery gales, and wall ties have to be doubly secure to prevent stems rubbing and chafing.

Thanks to the sunken dry moat, the east-facing façade of the Hall is able to support a considerable range of tender shrubs and climbers, but few average gardens can boast such a feature. If you despair of ever finding a plant to clothe your cold and windy east- or north-facing wall or fence, consider the following:

Chaenomeles (Japanese quince) Deciduous, twiggy, spring-flowering shrubs. They can be grown as free-standing specimens, but are best trained flat against a wall. Once a basic framework is formed, spur-prune sideshoots back to two or three buds after flowering. *C. speciosa* 'Moerloosei' is pink and white; *C. speciosa* 'Nivalis' is white and *C.* × *superba* 'Rowallane' is crimson.

Cotoneaster horizontalis A deciduous, spreading shrub with fan-like sprays of branches that are almost self-supporting. Bears tiny white flowers, beloved by bees, in spring, followed by bright red berries in autumn. For wall-trained specimens, remove any branches that are growing away from the support. *C. atropurpureus* 'Variegatus' (syn. *C. horizontalis* 'Variegatus') is an attractive cultivar with cream variegated leaves.

Hydrangea anomala **subsp.** *petiolaris* Deciduous, self-clinging climber with large, lacecap heads of white flowers in June and July. It is often slow to get started but will cover a huge area. Cut back unwanted growth after flowering. Old plants tolerate hard pruning.

Jasminum nudiflorum (winter jasmine) A deciduous, scandent shrub, producing bright yellow flowers on leafless stems throughout winter. Tie in the new long growths close against the wall, and cut back flowered shoots to within two or three buds of the framework.

Pyracantha (firethorn) A dense, spiny, evergreen shrub with white spring flowers followed by vibrant autumn berries. For wall-trained specimens, tie in shoots needed to form the framework, then after flowering cut back the lateral branches to two or three leaves to expose developing berries. Cultivars said to be resistant to pyracantha scab include red 'Mohave', yellow 'Soleil d'Or' and orange-red 'Orange Glow'.

Tips

● If the thought of scaling a ladder twice a year to prune your wisteria fills you with dread, you will probably welcome Owen's tip for dealing with this vigorous subject. 'We found out by accident that you can get away with pruning wisteria just once a year, not twice, as textbooks always recommend. After the hurricane in 1987, we got behind with all our maintenance jobs because there was so much felling and clearance work to be done. We eventually got round to pruning our wisteria in April and it flowered much better than ever before. By delaying the pruning till mid-spring, you can see exactly where the flower buds are and you remove all growth right up to those buds. This way you get the maximum amount of flowers but you also keep the plant under control.'

● Always make sure you use the right pruning tool for the job: secateurs for woody stems up to 1cm (0.5in) thick; long-handled loppers for branches no bigger than 2.5cm (1in) wide; and a pruning saw for anything larger. Always clean them with an oily rag after use and keep them sharp to avoid leaving a ragged wound on the plant.

● To prevent the deep, well-drained, loamy soil at Blickling becoming more acidic than it already is, Owen uses spent mushroom compost as a soil conditioner and mulch. This is lime-rich, and therefore alkaline, in nature so it helps to raise the pH of the soil, making it more accommodating for a wider range of plants.

Cotehele

CORNWALL

Area: 5·7ha (14 acres)
Soil: acid/loam
Altitude: 76m (250ft)
Average rainfall: 1,143mm
  (45in)
Average winter climate: mild

David Hingley, although now no longer with the National Trust, was Head Gardener at Cotehele for three years until 1997. Part of his contribution to the garden during that time was to tame the exuberant growth of many of the established plants, including the wall shrubs and climbers around the medieval house. 'The garden's informality appealed to me when I came here. I liked the way it seemed to have evolved to no particular plan,' he says. David has now gone on to work at Hodnet Hall Gardens in Shropshire, but his earlier horticultural posts included an eight-year spell in charge at another private garden, Kiftsgate Court, Gloucestershire, followed by seven years as Assistant Head Gardener at Killerton in Devon.

Climbers and wall plants at Cotehele

Climbing plants really only became a feature of the house walls at Cotehele when the National Trust took over the property in 1947; before that they supported nothing more exotic than ivy and Virginia creeper, according to old photographs. Now a host of tender and hardy subjects grace the granite faces of the outbuildings and of the medieval house. 'Everyone thinks that this is a sheltered Cornish valley garden, but that is far from the truth. When the wind comes from the north-east, it blows directly off Dartmoor, which you can see on the horizon, and funnels its way up the Valley Garden until it reaches the house. Therefore the east front can be very cold. Also the layout of the building, with all its courtyards and doorways, creates wind turbulence on certain corners, while others are prone to frosts, particularly where the sun never reaches,' explains David.

Taking advantage of the natural microclimates around the house is the key to success with climbers and wall shrubs at Cotehele. 'The beauty of the building is that we can accommodate a wide range of plants because the walls face every direction. For example, we have sunny, sheltered sites; sunny, windy ones; and shady, dry areas. Therefore I tailor the plant for the spot, rather than the other way round. The walls are pretty full now, so it's usually a matter of replacing dead or over mature plants,' he says. The lobster claw, *Clianthus puniceus*, and the scarlet trumpet vine, *Campsis radicans*, are sun-lovers and will only survive in the most sheltered sites, while camellias and *Berberidopsis corallina*, with its beads of crimson flowers suspended on long red stalks, do well in a moist, north-facing wall border in the Hall Court.

An arbour of *Robinia hispida*, which frames a view of the valley, makes an unusual feature on the edge of the East Terrace. 'It is certainly a talking point when it produces its chains of pea-like, pink flowers in late spring, but it is a pig of a plant to train because its stems are so brittle. Fortunately it makes lots of new growth every year, which is just as well because most of it will be snapped off when we come to tie it onto the framework.'

Shrubs suitable for wall-training

In a mild climate many so-called tender shrubs will grow happily as free-standing specimens in a border, but in cold districts their chances of survival will be substantially increased if you provide them with the protection of a wall. Depending on their habit and the available space, they may either be allowed to develop naturally, with nothing more than a light prune to keep them neat, or they can be formally trained and tied in as fans or espaliers. The wall also doubles as an attractive background for both flowers and foliage.

'We grow quite a number of tender wall shrubs in this garden. This is mainly achieved by intuitive guesswork and a bit of luck. I try to avoid those that require winter protection because they create too much work. There are times when I have abandoned a plant in preference for one which gives a similar effect purely for that reason,' David admits. The following are some of the wall shrubs that flourish at Cotehele, along with tips for pruning them. Unless stated otherwise, all are best in a sunny, sheltered position:

Abelia floribunda An evergreen shrub with arching shoots and small glossy leaves. Long, tubular, magenta flowers are produced in early summer. Trim lightly after flowering.

Azara **sp.** Evergreen shrubs from South America with sweetly scented, mimosa-like, yellow flowers, usually produced in winter or spring. Cut back shoots that have flowered to within two to four buds of the permanent framework to keep them within bounds.

Chimonanthus praecox **(wintersweet)** A deciduous shrub with glossy, mid-green foliage and fragrant, waxy, yellow flowers in winter on leafless stems. Immediately after flowering, cut back flowered shoots to within two to four buds of the permanent framework to keep them within bounds.

Clianthus puniceus An evergreen shrub with climbing shoots and vetch-like foliage. Showy, claw-like, scarlet flowers are produced from late spring to early summer. Cut back flowered shoots by about a third immediately after flowering. Keep it tight against the wall to prevent frost damage.

Clianthus puniceus albus

Fremontodendron californicum

Colquhounia coccinea An upright, evergreen sub-shrub with sage-green leaves and scarlet-orange flowers in late summer. Cut back flowered stems close to the base in early spring.

Crinodendron hookerianum A large, stiffly branched, evergreen shrub with small, pendant, lantern-shaped, deep red flowers in late spring. Likes acid soil and partial shade. After flowering, prune back shoots that spoil the plant's symmetry.

× *Fatshedera lizei* **'Variegata'** A spreading evergreen shrub with glossy, ivy-like foliage, which is heavily margined with creamy-white. In early spring remove misplaced shoots that spoil the plant's symmetry.

Fremontodendron californicum A vigorous, upright evergreen shrub with saucer-shaped, bright yellow flowers throughout summer. After flowering, cut back flowered shoots to within two to four buds of the permanent framework to keep them within bounds. Avoid contact with the foliage as it may irritate the skin and eyes.

Garrya elliptica **(silk-tassel bush)** A large, dense, evergreen shrub with dark green foliage and pendant, grey-green catkins produced from mid-winter to early spring. Male plants produce the best catkins. Good for partial or full shade in a position sheltered from cold winds. After flowering, remove the branches that spoil the plant's symmetry.

Sophora microphylla A spreading evergreen shrub with pinnate leaves and pea-like, dark yellow flowers in drooping clusters throughout spring. Best left unpruned.

Tweedia caerulea An evergreen scrambling sub-shrub with long, heart-shaped foliage and clusters of sky-blue flowers from summer to early autumn. Very tender, so needs cosseting in the warmest, sunniest, most sheltered spot available. May require winter protection, even in warm climates. In early spring cut back to within two to four buds of the permanent framework.

Vestia foetida An erect evergreen shrub with unpleasant-smelling, glossy foliage and pale yellow, fuchsia-like flowers from mid-spring to mid-summer. Trim lightly after flowering.

Vitex agnus-castus **(chaste tree)** A deciduous shrub with attractive, pointed, hand-shaped leaves and fragrant, purple-blue flower spikes in early autumn. In early spring cut right back to the permanent framework.

Renovation of neglected climbers and wall shrubs

One of David's main tasks at Cotehele was to tame the overgrown wall specimens. 'Many plants had become sorely neglected. Since I arrived, I seem to have done nothing but fell

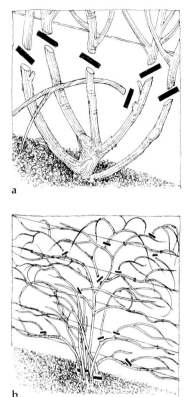

Two ways to renovate climbing plants – the drastic (**a**) and the cautious (**b**).

and prune. I think I am fast gaining a reputation as a philistine and vandal,' he laughs.

In the last three years matted jasmines, tangled climbing roses and a burgeoning *Wisteria sinensis* 'Alba' are just a few examples that have been subjugated by David. 'My main aim in pruning them hard is to generate new growth from lower down as well as to establish a framework which can be tied in flat against the wall. Apart from any other reason, it is a waste of a border if the plant has grown out too far.'

Some plants, like most of the jasmine tribe and many honeysuckles, respond well to drastic pruning – cutting back all the main stems to 30-60 cm (12-24 in) in one fell swoop (**a**). Others, such as wisteria and many evergreens, are best renovated in stages over several years, removing one in three of the main stems at a time (**b**). The following principles for renovation apply to both categories:

● Decide if your plant is worth renovating. If it is a diseased, weak or spindly specimen, it may be better to throw in the towel and start afresh with a healthy young plant.

● Most deciduous plants are best tackled in the dormant season, between November and February; evergreens should be pruned as they are coming into growth in spring.

● Prune out all weak, dead, diseased and damaged wood first.

● If you are unsure how the plant will respond to drastic pruning, err on the side of caution and cut back up to half of the oldest stems to just above ground level.

● Shorten the remaining stems by up to a half, or to either a vigorous young shoot or a healthy bud lower down. Tie in younger growth to fill gaps in the framework.

● Pamper the plant to help it recover from the shock by mulching around the base with garden compost or leafmould.

● Bear in mind it can take a number of years for your plant to regain its flowering stride, therefore consider annual climbers to temporarily cover ugly stumps and fill any gaps left by hard pruning. In the past David has grown *Cobaea scandens* and *Ipomoea lobata* (syn. *Mina lobata*) for this purpose.

Soil preparation and planting

Wherever possible, David prefers to plant wall shrubs and climbers in the autumn. Not only is the soil still warm, but the winter rains help to establish the plant before hot weather and summer droughts return. Old stumps and the roots of previous border occupants are removed, and the soil at the bottom of the planting hole is mixed with well-rotted farmyard manure or garden compost and a sprinkling of bonemeal. 'This slow-release fertiliser has the advantage of giving the plant an extra boost in the first few years to help cover the wall quickly, but then its effects wear off. I would not use anything stronger for fear of promoting too much growth which would have to be cut back constantly,' he explains.

Installing or renewing a framework of wires should be carried out at the planting stage. 'I start the wires about 90-120cm (3-4ft) above soil level; any lower than that, and they remain unused. Bamboo canes provide the initial support required to take stems to the first wire. How I train the plant depends on the available area. For instance, between two windows the plant will be restricted to a columnar shape, but where there is more space, I will fan out the growth as much as possible,' says David.

Watering is viewed as a temporary measure to help the plant establish itself in the first year. 'If I have to keep watering it, then I have probably chosen the wrong plant for that situation – which goes back to selecting climbers to suit the microclimate in the first place.'

Tips

Pea sticks make ideal supports for climbers against a wall and for those in the open border.

● Pea sticks make ideal toe-holds for scrambling plants such as the late-flowering clematis cultivars and rhodochiton. Use them in the open border or slide them beneath the wires on a wall. At the end of the season, simply cut down the plant, drag the whole lot out of the border and discard.

● Check permanent wall ties regularly to avoid damage to the trunk and branches of the plant as they increase in girth.

● Consider wiring the entire wall, rather than just individual plants. It will save time and effort in the long run and the overall effect will be far more natural – more of a woven tapestry than separate blocks of planting.

● Vet all bought-in stock carefully before you plant it in the garden. Vine weevil larvae are particularly troublesome on container-grown plants and are very difficult to eradicate. Look out for the tell-tale signs: the adult weevil makes notches around the margins of the leaves, while the creamy-coloured, comma-shaped grubs embedded in the compost will cause the wilting and eventual death of the plant stems and foliage. According to David, bantams are good at finding and picking out such soil-borne pests, but for those less inclined to keep poultry, the humble robin is the next best thing.

● If red spider mites are a problem on wall-trained plants in hot, dry summers, spray over the foliage regularly with a hose to increase the humidity around the plant.

Nymans

WEST SUSSEX

Area: 12ha (30 acres)
Soil: acid/sandy loam
Altitude: 152m (500ft)
Average rainfall: 762mm (30in)
Average winter climate: cold

The garden at Nymans has been in existence for just over a century. In that time, it has been looked after by only three head gardeners. The first was James Comber, who helped the owner, Ludwig Messel, create the garden; the second was Cecil Nice, who was in charge when the property passed to the National Trust in 1953. The third and present Head Gardener is David Masters, whose earlier career with the Trust has included working at Sheffield Park in East Sussex, followed by a spell as Head Gardener at Beningbrough Hall, North Yorkshire, before coming to Nymans in 1980.

Although much of the garden is made up of tree and shrub planting with extensive sweeps of grass, there are many labour-intensive areas which are bedded out at least once a season, and it is a tribute to David and his permanent staff of four and one trainee that these are maintained to such a high standard while major renovations and redevelopments still continue apace in other parts of the garden.

Climbers and wall plants at Nymans

Not only is Nymans particularly well endowed with walls, hedges and trees where all manner of climbers abound, but a variety of wooden and metal structures have also been installed to support yet more plants of scrambling, scandent or twining habit. 'Here at Nymans I have to walk a tricky tightrope between the relaxed and the scruffy. Some people would say that I have teetered into the scruffy, but I like to let the climbers have their head. Plants grow into each other and have to fight for space, but that is one of the characteristics of Nymans. You may well see climbers neatly fan-trained at other properties, but if all Trust gardens followed the same management principles, they would look much more alike,' says David.

Climbing plants play a significant role at Nymans for many, varied reasons:

To soften and enhance architectural features
The sense of profusion and giving plants their head is nowhere more apparent than on the walls of the ruined house, where the slightly out-of-control growth of climbers accentuates the romance and allure of the building, which in 1947 was reduced to a shell by fire. A venerable old *Wisteria floribunda* 'Multijuga' (syn. *W.* 'Macrobotrys') snakes its way along what is left of the south-west-facing wing, while more tender

climbers and wall shrubs such as *Magnolia grandiflora* and *Hydrangea serratifolia* (syn. *H. integerrima*), to name just two, bask in the shelter provided by the south-facing walls.

Similarly the delightful, clove-scented, pale pink climbing rose 'Blush Noisette' graces, but does not overwhelm, the dovecote, while the pure white, small-flowered 'Dundee Rambler' rose, together with blue-purple *Clematis* 'Jackmanii', flank the Italian loggia in the Sunk Garden. 'I am in two minds as to whether the summerhouse always benefits from this veil of plants. The automatic response of gardeners when faced with any building is to cover it with climbers. When the plants are in full foliage in summer, I think they actually detract from, rather than enhance the structure,' David admits.

To follow tradition

In a garden whose reputation in part has been built on grow-ing rarities such as *Lomatia tinctoria* from Tasmania and *Weinmannia trichosperma* from Chile, as well as introducing to cultivation plants hybridised at Nymans, including *Camellia* 'Leonard Messel' and *Magnolia* × *loebneri* 'Leonard Messel', the notion of continuity is important. 'Where appropriate, we try to replant with species that have been here over a period of time to maintain the feel and tradition of the garden,' he explains. For this reason many of the old rose cultivars, so beloved by Maud Messel in the 1920s, were re-propagated and put back in the renovated Rose Garden in 1988.

Similarly, this family link is retained in the Wall Garden where the perimeter borders follow a distinct, although by no means exclusive, Chilean theme. Primarily South American shrubs, such as *Azara integrifolia*, *Vestia foetida* and *Peumus boldus*, add structure and form, while tender climbers like lardizabala, eccremocarpus, berberidopsis and holboellia clothe the walls. Some are the original plants grown from seed collected by James Comber's son Harold in the 1920s; others are from more recent plant-hunting trips.

To screen off distinct areas

Even the most unobservant garden visitor could not fail to be aware of the definite trellis theme just beyond the reception area at Nymans, inspired mainly by the curious white kiosk-like building, which has now been placed adjacent to the tea-room and shop. In this small area variously sized trellis perform several functions. Not only does it create a feeling of protection and enclosure, it also helps to form visual barriers. For example, the tall grey-stained trellis does a fine job of screening the car park from the garden, heightening the sense of anticipation when you first arrive. Sometimes referred to as a 'fedge', since it resembles both hedge and fence, its veil of Virginia creeper and blue, spring-flowering *Clematis macropetala* provide two seasons of interest. Shorter white trellis, which support large-flowered hybrid clematis such as the velvety-blue 'Countess of Lovelace', help demarcate the display bays in the sales area.

To hide eyesores

Wonderful for rearing plants it may be, but the recently erected all-singing, all-dancing glasshouse at Nymans is a definite no-no in terms of fitting into its environment. 'It somehow did not seem quite right to be confronted by 1990s technology when you step out of a beautiful 1920s rose garden,' laughs David. For this reason it was decided to erect a temporary trellis, about 2·4 m (8 ft) tall, parallel to the longest side of the greenhouse. A beech hedge, already making good growth on the fertile sandy loam, will in time replace the screen which is planted with the sweetly scented but small-flowered *Lonicera japonica* 'Halliana'.

To provide two seasons of interest

In a garden which comes under the scrutiny of eagle-eyed visitors throughout the opening season, the idea of extending the flowering interest by packing twice as many plants into the same amount of space comes as naturally as breathing to most head gardeners. Fortunately this jumbled style of planting, which is evident throughout the garden, suits Nymans down to the ground. Just a few of the many examples include late summer-flowering *Clematis flammula* which play centre stage in the Rose Garden after mid-summer rambler roses take to the wings, and the purple pompons of *Clematis viticella* 'Purpurea Plena Elegans' which steals the show in the Wall Garden after the white *Hydrangea anomala* subsp. *petiolaris*, has bowed out in July.

To produce complementary plant associations

Sometimes the above philosophy is abandoned in favour of a double helping of simultaneous flower colour, which though shorter-lived, certainly packs a punch in terms of its visual impact. For instance, the blue potato blooms of *Solanum crispum* 'Glasnevin' make a wonderful foil for the blowsy white *Clematis* 'Huldine', while the nodding, rose-pink bells of *C.* 'Etoile Rose' contrast particularly well with the scarlet and magenta flowers of *Fuchsia* 'Voltaire'.

To introduce height in a border

Most planting schemes benefit from a certain amount of height at the back of the border, not only to help anchor them within their site but also to act as a visual full stop. At Nymans tall rustic tripods, made from bean poles, have been erected at intervals along the length of the summer borders, and are planted mainly with large-flowered hybrids such as C. 'Jackmanii' and C.'Lilacina Floribunda'. After growth reaches the top, it spreads out sideways onto pea sticks, positioned primarily to support lofty herbaceous perennials, thereby creating a luxuriant, flowering curtain from July to October.

Pruning wisteria

There are a number of wisteria at Nymans. Come late spring, *W. floribunda* 'Multijuga', with its long, dripping, lilac-blue racemes, makes a breathtaking sight on the walls of the ruin, as well as cascading over the 20-m (60-ft) long pergola on the west side of the croquet lawn. Both are thought to be around the same age, having been planted about 1904. Because they are so old and large, they are almost self-regulating, making little extension growth but still flowering with great gusto, therefore David prefers not to interfere with them. However, this is not the case with the twelve-year-old *W. floribunda* 'Alba', draped over the garden shed, which is rigorously spur-pruned twice a year. If your wisteria fails to live up to your expectations, David advocates the following regime:

● In the early years concentrate your efforts on simply tying in new growth until the plant has reached the desired size and adequately covers the supporting structure. The idea of pruning is to maintain the basic framework once it has formed (**a**).

● Once established, prune the wisteria in July, cutting back all the long bright green laterals and sideshoots to within about six leaves of the main framework. This will retain a good leaf cover for the summer to feed the plant but will also restrict its vigour (**b**).

● In February prune back the laterals and sideshoots to within about two or three buds of the framework. This will help encourage flower formation for the coming season (**c**).

Pruning wisteria.

a

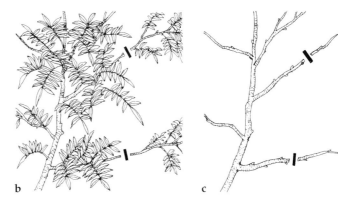

b   c

Growing annual climbers from seed

It is a joy to see row upon row of sturdy little plants, bright green and full of promise, lined out neatly in trays on the floor of the large glasshouse at Nymans. This is the domain of Alex Mawson, who has been propagator here for two years. As well as supplying David with all the annuals he requires for the summer borders, she also grows a good number of annual climbers destined for the trellis near the entrance of the garden. She recommends the following method for propagating annuals such as *Tropaeolum canariensis*, *Cobaea scandens*, *Ipomoea lobata* (syn. *Mina lobata*), *Ipomoea* 'Heavenly Blue' and *Eccremocarpus scaber*:

● Sow large seed such as tropaeolum and ipomoea in individual plugs or small pots in early April using a peat-based sowing compost. Cover the seed to about its own depth with vermiculite, and water in with a copper-based fungicide to reduce the incidence of damping off.

● Sow small seed such as eccremocarpus in a seed tray, sprinkling it thinly over the surface of the compost. Cover with a fine layer of vermiculite.

● At Nymans, the seeds are then placed on a heated mist bench to germinate, but for those with less sophisticated facilities, watering the compost carefully before placing a sheet of glass and newspaper over the container, should assure equal success. Maintain a temperature of 16–20°C (61–68°F).

● After germination when the seedlings are large enough to handle, pot up or prick-out into 9-cm (3.5-in) or 12.5-cm (5-in) pots, depending on the available space. Alex uses a peat and bark-based compost, to which she adds slow-release fertiliser and water-retaining granules. Stake as necessary.

● Harden off fully and plant out during the third or fourth week in May when all risk of frost is over.

Pruning rambler roses on arches and pillars

Mention Nymans, and it is usually not long before roses crop up in the conversation. Although rambler roses are used throughout the garden, they also make a dominant feature in the Rose Garden, where they have been thoughtfully trained to look almost as good out of flower as they do blooming their hearts out.

On the free-standing pillars in the middle of the beds new growth is twisted round like a cork-screw. 'I did this on the basis that the longer the stem, the more flower is likely to be produced. If it is tied in vertically, it might grow to 2.7m (9ft) until it reaches the top of the support, but training it spirally gives an extra metre or so of growth. Anyway, the more horizontally you can train them, the better roses flower,' explains David. In autumn the whole plant is untied from the pillar and laid out on the ground. The oldest growth is cut right out at the base and the newest is tied in to bamboo canes, which are secured at an angle on the framework.

The ramblers on the metal arches are treated slightly differently. If the rose naturally produces plenty of new growth near the base, it is trained vertically like the strings of a guitar, while all the old stems are totally removed. However, others like the coppery-pink 'Paul Transon', are less obliging, and make all their new wands near the top. David has tried training these downwards with varying success, but admits the only way to regenerate such a rose is to cut out about a third of the oldest stems to ground level.

Recommended ramblers and vigorous climbers for arches and pillars include:

'Albéric Barbier' Creamy white, ageing to pure white; semi-evergreen; 5m (15ft)

'Goldfinch' Deep yellow, fading to creamy white; 4m (12ft)

'New Dawn' Whitish-pink blooms from summer to autumn; climber to 3m (10ft)

'Phyllis Bide' Coppery-pink flowers from summer to autumn; climber to 3m (10ft)

'Sanders' White Rambler' Sprays of small white flowers in late summer; 4m (12ft)

'Veilchenblau' Violet blooms streaked with white; 4m (12ft)

'Violette' Flowers opening reddish-purple, fading to greyish-mauve; 4m (12ft)

Propagating rambler roses

Most rambler roses, and many other cultivars that are closely related to wild species, are very easy to propagate from hardwood cuttings because they do not require special facilities or equipment to form roots.

● Prepare the cutting bed by digging over the soil, removing any weeds and breaking up large clods.

● In October remove from the parent plant well-ripened shoots of about pencil thickness in diameter. Ideally these should not have produced flowers during the summer, but if they have, simply cut them off.

● Prepare the cuttings by removing the leaves, the soft tip wood and any spent flowers.

● Cut into lengths, each measuring about 30cm (12in). To remind you which way up to insert the cutting, make an

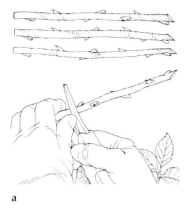

a

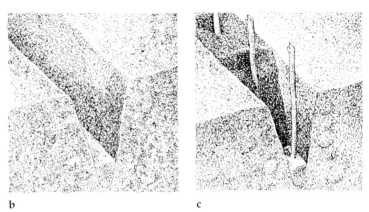

b   **c**

Propagating rambler roses from hardwood cuttings.

angled cut above the top bud and a straight cut below the bottom bud. Dip the base in hormone rooting powder (**a**).

● Take out a narrow V-shaped trench about 15cm (6in) deep in the prepared cutting bed. Trickle a little coarse sand along the bottom to increase drainage and encourage rooting (**b**).

● Insert the cuttings vertically to about two-thirds of their length, 15cm (6in) apart along the trench, ensuring each one makes contact with the sand (**c**).

● Replace the soil, firm in, water well and label the cuttings.

● Roots should form the following spring, and by autumn the young plants can be lifted carefully and transplanted to their permanent positions.

Creating a curtain-effect using climbers

Erecting trelliswork is a very useful way of camouflaging eyesores and screening off distinct areas, but it tends to look rather obvious. As a less heavy solution, David has created a simple T-shaped framework of wires to 'lose' the unappealing administration building beneath a veil of *Vitis coignetiae* 'Claret Cloak.' The single vertical strand of wire supports the climber in the early stages until an almost self-supporting woody trunk is formed, while the horizontal wire at the top lends support to the long laterals from which sideshoots grow and hang down like a living curtain. Only three strong leaders are allowed to grow from the base: one to grow in each direction along the gutter line, the other kept as an insurance policy in case one fails.

For ease of maintenance to the structure beneath, the upright wire slopes towards the building at the top. Strainers, fixed to a strong bracket at gutter level and set in concrete about 25cm (10in) away from the base, help keep the wire taut. The plant is set out an extra 20cm (8in) away to avoid the rain shadow created beneath the eaves of the building.

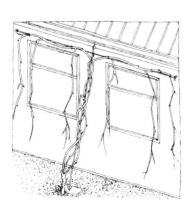

Vitis coignetiae trained to create a living curtain.

Tips

● Use coloured preservative rather than paint for timber and trelliswork in the garden. It comes in a wide range of complementary shades to suit most planting schemes, and does not need to be applied as frequently – an obvious boon if you have ever tried painting a piece of white trellis beneath a favourite plant which you are loathe to cut down.

● If you fancy growing a rambler rose up a hedge or a tree, ensure the host plant is man enough to take it. Avoid the lovely but brutish *R. filipes* 'Kiftsgate', which can reach a lofty 10m (30ft), unless you have a well-established tree such as oak or holly to provide the necessary competition. Established apple or pear trees make far more suitable partners for less vigorous ramblers such as 'Goldfinch' or 'Sanders' White Rambler', which only grow to about 4m (12ft).

● Although we generally plant climbers to head for the heights, many will be equally happy to live on the flat where they make unusual groundcover specimens. Honeysuckles, tropaeolums, such as the flame-red *Tropaeolum speciosum*, and some of the more vigorous clematis species are ideal candidates for this soil-hugging position. One of the most successful examples of this can be found in the Wall Garden, where David has planted a mat of creamy yellow *Lonicera periclymenum* 'Graham Thomas' beneath *Magnolia campbellii*.

● Similarly, many shrubs, more commonly grown as free-standing specimens, can be fanned out to make novel wall climbers. At Nymans, the Russian sage, *Perovskia atriplicifolia*, looks very effective trained in this fashion, but David also recommends the white *Viburnum plicatum* 'Sterile', which grows in this way at nearby Sissinghurst.

● If you do not want to set the base of metal arches in concrete, you can sink them straight into the ground to a depth of about 60cm (24in), which should hold them firm. Locate the exact position of the arch and make holes to the appropriate depth by driving in a T-shaped piece of metal with the same dimensions as the metal supports. Remove carefully, slide the metal structure into position and re-firm the soil.

● Some climbers can be trained to produce almost topiary-like effects. For example, on the main lawn a veritable 'flower basket', in existence since Victorian times, has recently been restored, using winter jasmine to represent the basket, and red-flowered hydrangeas to signify the contents. The jasmine, which incidentally still produces a fine display of bright yellow winter flowers, is tied to the basket-shaped framework and clipped several times a year to maintain a crisp outline.

Penrhyn Castle

GWYNEDD

Area: 19ha (47 acres)
Soil: neutral/sandy and stony
Altitude: 46m (150ft)
Average rainfall: 1,092mm
    (43in)
Average winter climate: mild

The current Head Gardener at Penrhyn and inheritor of the horticultural mantle of the formidable Victorian Walter Speed (see p.12) is Mike Anderson. While Speed was expected to supply the family of the big house, no matter where they were in the country, with daily fresh fruit and vegetables from the kitchen garden, Mike has to ensure the forty-seven acres of garden meet the high expectations of an increasingly fastidious public throughout the six-month visiting season. With a total staff of just three, that is no mean feat.

Giving up a career in engineering at the age of 21 to pursue his interest in horticulture, Mike worked for his local Parks Department and Health Authority before joining the Trust at Penrhyn Castle in 1979. About ten years later he was promoted to Head Gardener. 'Like everyone, I have good and bad days at work. But if things get to me, I just remind myself of how it was before I came here, when I lived for Friday nights and weekends. Although there are tight budget constraints within the National Trust, it is nothing compared to the world I've left behind which existed on less than a shoestring, where areas were simply put down to grass through lack of finances,' he says ruefully.

Climbers and wall plants at Penrhyn

Much of the pleasure ground around the castle is made up of sweeps of grass punctuated by fine ornamental trees and shrubs, but a short distance away to the west lies a small walled garden where the mood changes entirely. Intimate in scale, with the top terrace laid out as a formal box-edged parterre, it is intensively cultivated, and forms a striking contrast to the surrounding woodland. Within this sheltered enclosure all manner of tender plants flourish, not only profiting from its high brick walls in particular, but also benefiting from the warming effects of the Gulf Stream in general.

Mike appreciates the fact that he is lucky enough to have the sort of conditions many gardeners would give their eye-teeth for, and at Penrhyn he exploits this to the full. 'Often we go by what we know works, but at the same time there is always room to experiment. Sometimes it works and pays off, sometimes it doesn't. As long as we keep mainly to the overall theme of a Victorian garden and pleasure ground, we have quite a free rein in our choice of plants and the way we arrange them,' he explains.

Mike is also very much aware that every Trust garden

should have its own identity to prevent them all becoming too similar. 'In many ways we are still developing our own character. That is why we are trying to grow a different range of plants visitors are unlikely to see elsewhere.'

Given such a favourable climate, the tendency to try out ever more tender and exotic species must be overwhelming. But as Mike points out, over-zealousness must be tempered by pragmatism and a sense of restraint. 'It is important to have a balance of tender and hardy species. If we go overboard and plant too many delicate climbers, they would simply get neglected because we do not have the time to give them the attention they require,' he explains.

Climbers for a mild climate

Listed below are some of the climbers and wall shrubs that fare particularly well at Penrhyn, with Mike's comments and his pruning techniques:

Fremontodendron californicum An evergreen shrub producing large buttercup-like, golden flowers throughout summer. 'Best left to develop naturally until its overall shape is established. Then prune the long shoots back to within two to four buds of the main framework in early spring. Contact with the foliage may irritate the skin. Avoid this by covering the eyes and wearing gloves when pruning.'

Jasminum mesnyi A slender evergreen shrub producing large, semi-double, bright yellow flowers in spring and summer. 'Although supposedly tender, we have found it comes through well here. Treat like the common winter jasmine and prune out all flowered wood soon after flowering. Tie in new growth.'

Jasminum polyanthum A tender evergreen climber bearing masses of highly scented, white flowers from spring to summer. 'Requires little regular pruning other than to thin out overcrowded growth after flowering.'

Lapageria rosea A twining evergreen climber bearing long, bell-shaped, waxy, pinkish-red flowers from summer to late autumn. 'Here it enjoys a long flowering season right up to December. Grow in acid soil in partial shade. Best left unpruned, although you can cut out unwanted or badly placed growth in early spring.'

Mitraria coccinea A scandent evergreen shrub producing showy, tubular, scarlet flowers from late spring to autumn. 'Keep the roots cool and shaded in acid soil but allow the top to scramble up to grow in sun. It likes the protection of neighbouring plants. Trim lightly in mid-spring to keep it within bounds.'

Lapageria rosea

Mutisia spinosa **var.** *pulchella* A suckering climber with small, dark green leaves that are woolly beneath. 'It likes to grow with its feet in shade and its head in sun. Its abundant daisy-like, clear pink flowers are followed by attractive seed-heads a bit like old man's beard, so it provides two seasons of interest. To restrict its size, trim lightly in spring.'

Solanum crispum **'Glasnevin'** A fast-growing, semi-evergreen climber producing starry, blue flowers with pointed yellow centres, rather like potato flowers, from summer to autumn. 'To prevent it getting too unwieldy, fan out and tie in the main branches, then spur-prune the laterals back to three or four buds of this permanent framework in late winter.'

Solanum jasminoides **'Album'** A scrambling, semi-evergreen climber bearing blue-tinged, white potato flowers from summer to autumn. 'At Penrhyn it does not seem to be at all tender. Prune in the same way as *S. crispum*.'

Sollya heterophylla A twining evergreen climber with small bell-shaped, blue flowers from early summer to autumn. Spur-prune the sideshoots back to three or four buds of the framework in early spring. 'This is a tender climber we have lost before, so now we give it winter protection.'

Stauntonia hexaphylla A fast-growing, frost-hardy, evergreen climber with scented, violet-tinged, white flowers in spring, and sometimes edible purple fruits in autumn. 'As it is a vigorous, twining climber, we grow it up through *Fraxinus ornus*, or Chinese ash, which can bear its weight. I do not prune it at all.'

Propagating from semi-ripe cuttings

Little propagation is practised at Penrhyn, but on the odd occasion when it is necessary, semi-ripe cuttings are usually taken from mid- to late summer. Mike recommends the following method for many climbers, including berberidopsis, jasmine, mutisia, schisandra, schizophragma, solanum, stauntonia and trachelospermum:

● Remove from the parent plant healthy, well-developed, non-flowering shoots which are not fully hardened. They should be about 10–15cm (4–6in) long.

● With a sharp knife remove the lower leaves, cutting flush with the stem, and trim below a leaf axil. Alternatively, take a 'heel' by gently pulling the shoot away from the parent plant so that a small section of bark is also removed. Trim the heel slightly and treat with hormone rooting powder.

● Insert the cuttings into a pot or pan containing a 50:50 mixture of sharp sand and peat substitute.

Solanum jasminoides 'Album'

● Water thoroughly, then place in a propagator to root. At Penrhyn Mike uses a simple makeshift propagating box, which has a lid covered with a sheet of polythene, and positions this in an unheated glasshouse.

● Some species such as mutisia form roots within five weeks, others may take considerably longer. Once rooted, pot up individually and grow on until large enough to plant out.

Propagation by layering

By their very nature, most climbers produce long, trailing stems, which are more often than not tied to vertical supports. However, the gardener can exploit this natural snaking tendency to produce new plants by a process known as layering. Some, like ivy, mitraria and solanum, obligingly do this of their own accord, but many others, such as clematis, lapageria, mutisia and wisteria, require a little encouragement. Mike offers the following advice:

● In spring lightly cultivate the surrounding soil, forking in some organic matter to produce a crumbly tilth.

● Choose a healthy, well-placed shoot which is long enough to trail along the ground, and peg it down firmly in the prepared area using U-shaped pieces of wire. Cover with about 5-8cm (2-3in) of soil (a).

● Alternatively, before pegging down the shoot, carefully make a small incision on the underside of the stem close to each node. This wound is meant to encourage root formation although Mike has found that this procedure makes little difference to the overall result (b).

● By autumn roots should have formed, in which case the shoot can be lifted carefully and severed close to the parent plant. Like the NHS, Mike needs all the bed space he can get, so he removes the young plants as soon as possible.

● Separate the plantlets, cutting away any pieces of the old stem, before potting them up individually (c).

Layering climbers.

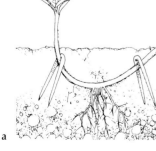

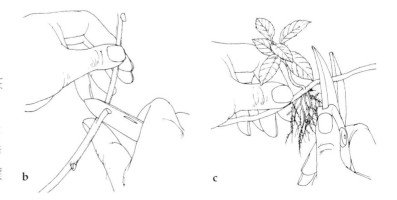

a
b
c

● Overwinter in a cold frame, pot on and stake as necessary. Plant out the following autumn.

Winter protection

In a garden where much of the flowering interest relies on plants of borderline hardiness, providing winter protection might be considered an overriding factor for most gardeners. Not so with Mike. 'Where I can, I try to avoid over-protecting the plants because I want to toughen them up. My main aim is to reduce the degree of frost, rather than exclude it altogether.'

Young plants and very tender subjects such as sollya require the most cosseting. Mike erects a simple frame around the plant, made from bamboo canes, and covers it with wind-break netting. 'I prefer not to pad this out with straw as textbooks recommend because I think it makes the growth too soft. If we get a hard frost when the protection is removed, usually at the beginning of February, then the plant suffers all the more,' he says.

Physiological drought

At Penrhyn pests and diseases are not particularly irksome, but a phenomenon known as physiological drought is more of a problem. Curiously it occurs when there is plenty of water in the soil but the plant cannot take it up fast enough to replace the moisture lost from the leaves as they transpire. Warm drying winds and frozen soil are both common causes. 'We find evergreens are most prone to this. One year severe frost locked the ground solid for about five weeks. All we could do was offer the plants partial shade from the burning effects of the sun and protection from the worst of the wind. We then cut out all damaged growth in spring,' Mike explains. There is no way of avoiding physiological drought, but problems can be mitigated by practising good husbandry and discouraging soft, fleshy growth late in the season.

Fuchsia arch

The microclimate at Penrhyn allows orthodox plants to be used in unorthodox ways. For example, one of the highlights within the Walled Garden is the fuchsia arch. Stretching across most of the long walk, it is planted with the hardy *Fuchsia* 'Riccartonii', which forms an intimate tunnel dripping with delicate scarlet and purple flowers from mid-summer until the first frosts. Add to this a dash of clematis, in the form of white 'Marie Boisselot' (syn. 'Madame le Coultre') and velvet purple 'Jackmanii Superba', and you have one of the most breathtaking spectacles to be seen in any garden.

Extending about 100m (330ft), it boasts about 60 hooped,

wrought-iron arches, with a more ornate ogee arch at either end. At the top, four thin metal crosspieces span its entire length to give rigidity, while thin green wire has been strung across from each upright to support lateral growth at the sides. Not only is the fuchsia arch particularly attractive, but it is also a very useful means of dividing up the garden. Neither as dense as a hedge nor as solid as a wall, it changes with the seasons, and because the spaces between the uprights act as 'windows', it allows tantalising glimpses to the Stream Garden below, created by Lady Penrhyn in the 1920s.

Creating a fuchsia arch

If you live in a sheltered area and would like to try growing a fuchsia and clematis walkway in your own garden, Mike offers the following tips:

● Erect the arches as necessary, sinking them into concrete to hold them firm.

● In spring, plant one fuchsia and one clematis, approximately 45 cm (18 in) apart, about 30-45 cm (12-18 in) outside each upright (**a**). For ease of maintenance, choose from the available range of late-flowering clematis cultivars, which require a similar pruning regime to the fuchsias.

● For the first few winters protect the young fuchsias using windbreak netting. 'The plants will lose their foliage, but the stems should remain in good heart,' says Mike.

● Once the fuchsias have become established, usually after about three or four seasons, prune them at the end of March, or later in less sheltered areas.

● Reduce the number of stems by about half, cutting out the weakest to ground level, and tying in the remainder to the supporting structure (**b**). If a hard winter seemingly kills the plant, do not despair: cut down all the dead stems and new shoots should erupt from the base in spring.

How to create a fuchsia and clematis arch: the plants in relation to the framework (**a**); reducing the established fuchsia stems by about half in late March (**b**); and pruning the clematis to about head height in early March (**c**).

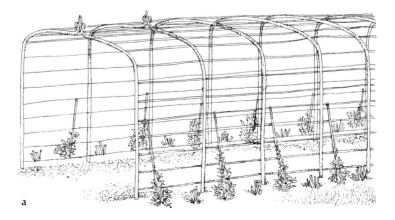

a

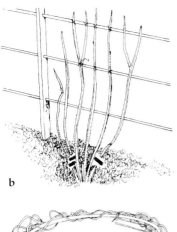

b

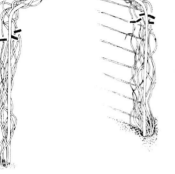

c

● In early March prune back the clematis to a permanent framework, about 1·5m (5ft) above the ground (**c**).

● To retain a loose but tidy column of growth, pull in the fuchsia branches and secure them with garden twine. You may have to do this several times throughout the summer, depending on the vigour of the plants.

● In March or April apply a sprinkling of bonemeal for healthy growth, followed by a generous mulch of leafmould to conserve soil moisture.

Tips

● Get to know your climbers and ensure you give them enough space to grow. It is all too tempting to cram in just one more, since many, like clematis, seem to thrive on the shoulders of others. However, less thuggish subjects, such as trachelospermum, prefer a bit of breathing space as they can become choked very easily.

● Choose the right plant for the particular situation. For instance, do not plant a climber that needs full sun on a north-facing wall. Similarly one that requires shelter is doomed to failure in a windy spot.

● Do not be afraid to experiment with climbers. If you know the garden's soil and aspect suit your chosen climber, by all means give it a go. Even in cold gardens sheltered micro-climates – for example, against south-facing house walls – can make the difference between success and failure.

Sizergh Castle

CUMBRIA

Area: 6·5 ha (16 acres)
Soil: neutral/shallow loam
  overlying limestone
Altitude: 61 m (200 ft)
Average rainfall: 1,270 mm
  (50 in)
Average winter climate: mild–
  moderate

Malcolm Hutcheson has been Head Gardener at Sizergh Castle since 1970. 'At the time, I was looking to leave Falkirk Parks Department, and the National Trust seemed to be a good organisation to work for. Although the salary here was little more than I was earning, it was the promise of gaining control of that lovely rock garden which sold the place to me,' he recalls. Fortunately, Malcolm had valuable experience of alpines from the Royal Botanic Gardens, Kew, where he began his horticultural career. Sizergh has also proved the ideal property in which to indulge his abiding love of flora and fauna. 'Gardening is my career and natural history is my hobby; the two blend very nicely here,' he says, clearly besotted by the place. When he reels off the list of unusual wildlife to be found on the estate – red squirrels, hawfinches and rare butterflies – it is hard to remain unmoved by his enthusiasm.

He is immensely proud of the fact that eight species of native orchid have moved in by themselves, and are now thriving on the south-facing banks below the castle, along with many other wild flowers and bulbs. He puts this down to correct management of the site. 'I delay cutting the grass until late summer, by which time the flowers have set seed. I then remove all the clippings to impoverish the soil and prevent vigorous grasses becoming established.'

Climbers and wall plants at Sizergh Castle

Until the last few years, the climate of this northerly garden has always been mild and moist, both in summer and winter, but Malcolm feels this is definitely on the change, with more prolonged periods of frost making their presence felt even into May. 'We have lost much of our rainfall. Even when there is cloud to the west and fog to the south, Sizergh is often in bright sunshine, a bit like a "sun sandwich",' he jokes.

Naturally this shift in the weather pattern has had an impact on the plants that can be grown, and the practice of exploiting favourable microclimates within the garden has become more important and pertinent than ever. Tender climbers and shrubs take full advantage of the garden's more sheltered spots. For example, the self-clinging *Pileostegia viburnoides* and *Hydrangea seemannii*, both of which are evergreen with whitish flowers, nestle at the base of the castle walls, while figs, *Buddleja crispa*, *Itea ilicifolia* and *Teucrium fruticans*, to name but a few, bask in the warm, free-draining conditions on the raised terrace that runs adjacent to the high, south-facing stone wall, which is faced with red brick to retain the heat.

The range of climbers that tolerate the shadier conditions in the courtyard at the back of the castle is less extensive. Those that flourish include the self-supporting *Hydrangea anomala* subsp. *petiolaris*, schizophragma and *Parthenocissus tricuspidata*, more commonly known as Boston ivy; pink *Rosa* 'Zéphirine Drouhin' and soft yellow *Lonicera periclymenum* 'Graham Thomas' add jabs of summer colour.

To extend the period of interest many of the established trees at Sizergh play host to a variety of climbers. The expansive white rambler *Rosa mulliganii* (syn. *R. longicuspis*) is a popular choice against the sombre, dark green foliage of the yew trees in the area to the west of the castle, while a single plant of the roving *Fallopia baldschuanica* (syn. *Polygonum baldschuanicum*), the aptly named mile-a-minute vine, presently drapes itself over a large yew tree as well as a Corsican pine to the south-east. 'As you can see, it would not be the ideal choice for a small garden, but where it has the space, it produces a wonderful waterfall of white flowers throughout August,' laughs Malcolm.

Climbers and wall plants from hardwood cuttings

Malcolm is the first to admit that he enjoys propagating plants of any kind, but especially those that come from wild-collected stock, whether indigenous to this country or native of somewhere further afield. 'I'm a species man myself. If I find a plant interesting, I like to try to propagate it, no matter what it is. I love the challenge of it all,' he says enthusiastically.

At Sizergh he has a range of propagating facilities at his disposal, including several glasshouses and coldframes. 'I take quite a lot of hardwood cuttings, which I insert directly into the soil of a coldframe. Although I do use heat inside the glasshouse, I think it is this cold culture, which is quite an old-fashioned system, that sets us apart here,' says Malcolm. Hardwoods may be slow to root sometimes, but he favours this method because it is straightforward and the cuttings are easy to maintain in a healthy condition. Many deciduous subjects such as climbing hydrangea, buddleja and climbing and rambler roses can be propagated in this way after their leaves have fallen, but it is also useful for some evergreens, for example hebe, escallonia and cistus.

● Prepare the base of the coldframe by spreading a thick layer of coarse gravel at the bottom for drainage. Cover with a 23cm (9in) layer of compost, comprising of a mix of 50:50 peat substitute and coarse sand.

● Take hardwood cuttings at the beginning of the dormant period from October to November using healthy shoots that have become woody during the current season.

● Remove lengths of stem, measuring about 15cm (6in), from the parent plant, cutting just above a bud.

● On each cutting, make a sloping cut just above the top bud and a horizontal cut below the bottom one. Apply hormone rooting powder to the basal cut only.

● Insert the cuttings directly into the coldframe about 10-15cm (4-6in) apart, in rows about 10cm (4in) apart. Leave about 2·5cm (1in) of the cutting above the soil surface.

● Label, water well and close the coldframe. Ventilate in warm weather.

● Most hardwood cuttings should have formed roots by the following spring, or autumn at the latest, when they can be potted up and grown on.

Propagating clematis from seed

Malcolm finds the best way of increasing most of his clematis species, such as *C. flammula*, *C. macropetala*, *C. potaninii* var. *potaninii* and the herbaceous *C. recta*, is from seed.

● If you are collecting your own clematis seed, harvest it when it is immature or 'green' to avoid the development of dormancy and speed up germination. If left on the parent plant too long, the seed dries and ripens, and only a period of chilling will break its inbuilt dormancy.

● Sow the seeds, complete with their fluffy 'tails', in a pot or tray containing firmed, moist, gritty seed compost (**a**).

● Just cover the seeds with a layer of compost, then sprinkle over a shallow layer of fine grit. Not only does this prevent the compost drying out, but it will keep the seeds well aerated and make it easy to remove weeds (**b**).

● Label the container, water with a fine spray to avoid displacing the seed, and plunge in a coldframe to germinate.

● Prick out into individual pots once seedlings have developed their first pair of true leaves. Place in the coldframe to grow on, staking the new shoots as necessary.

● Plant out into their permanent positions when they are well established and fully hardened off.

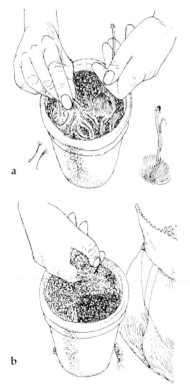

a

b

Propagating clematis from seed.

Propagating clematis from leaf-bud cuttings

Named clematis cultivars do not come true from seed and are therefore best propagated from leaf-bud, or internodal, cuttings taken in July. This can be achieved in two ways:

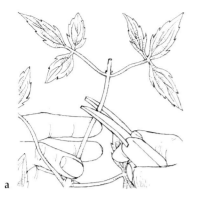

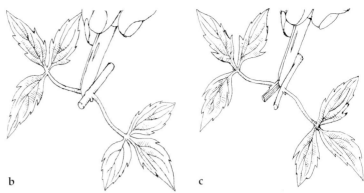

a

b

c

Taking leaf-bud cuttings from clematis.

● First make a cut just above a node and trim the stem to 2·5-5 cm (1-2 in) below it.

● Then either remove one of the pair of leaves (**b**), or split the stem cleanly down the middle to produce two cuttings (**c**).

● Treat the cut surfaces with hormone rooting powder and insert into a pot of cutting compost with the bud just above the compost surface. Firm gently and water in with a fungicide.

● Place either in a coldframe or in a heated greenhouse to root; those in the latter will probably form roots quicker.

Crevice plants

Although they cannot be described as wall shrubs or climbers, there are plants that grow *in* rather than on or against walls. These are known as crevice plants, and they are particularly abundant at Sizergh, where the ancient stone walls, together with their often crumbling mortar, is tailor-made for such opportunists. At the base of the castle a trio of attractive colonising species vie for attention; the small native fern *Asplenium trichomanes*, or maidenhair spleenwort, makes the perfect evergreen foil for the white and pink, daisy-like *Erigeron karvinskianus* (syn. *E. mucronatus*) and the diminutive, bright pink *Erinus alpinus*.

The easiest, and often best, plants for crevices in walls and paving will be those that find their own way there, their seeds successfully germinating in the tiniest amount of soil. To encourage this natural proclivity, establish the plant of your choice in a border nearby, then sit back and watch the results. Within a season or two its offspring will be popping up all around – all you need do is pull out seedlings where they are not wanted.

Other candidates for cracks and crevices include:

Armeria maritima **(sea thrift)** A small, clump-forming, ever-green perennial with grassy foliage and rounded, pink flowerheads from late spring to summer. Grows to 20cm (8in).

Asplenium scolopendrium (syn. *Phyllitis scolopendrium*) A glossy, evergreen fern with long, pointed, tongue-shaped leaves. Grows to 45–70cm (18–28in).

Aubrieta deltoidea A carpet-forming, evergreen perennial with four-petalled flowers in shades of white, pink, mauve and purple appearing in spring. Grows to 5cm (2in).

Aurinia saxatilis 'Citrina' (syn. *Alyssum saxatile* var. *citrinum*) An evergreen, mound-forming perennial with grey-green leaves and abundant small lemon-yellow flowerheads from late spring to early summer. Grows to 20cm (8in).

Campanula portenschlagiana A mound-forming evergreen perennial with funnel-shaped, deep purple flowers that appear from mid- to late summer. Grows to 15cm (6in). *C. poscharskyana* is similar but more vigorous, with star-shaped, bluish-mauve flowers.

Centranthus ruber (valerian) A woody-based perennial with mid-green leaves and reddish-pink flowerheads from late spring to late summer. Grows to 90cm (3ft).

Meconopsis cambrica (Welsh poppy) A tap-rooted perennial with shallow, cup-shaped yellow or orange flowers from spring to autumn. Grows to 45cm (18in).

Replanting a wall border

By their very nature, gardens are in a constant state of change; plants grow and borders mature. It is the gardener's job to direct the individual performers in this play: a snip or maybe full-scale removal here, an introduction to fill a gap there. However, there usually comes a time when a total face-lift is called for; the south-facing wall border on the raised terrace at Sizergh recently reached that point.

Out have gone the old over-mature shrubs and climbers, and in has come fresh young stock. As it is such a prime site, the emphasis is still on tender subjects such as *Lomatia myricoides*, with its unusual narrow, toothed foliage and elegant white flowers, and *Romneya coulteri*, with its glaucous foliage and crêpe paper-like, white petals surrounding a central boss of prominent, golden stamens. However, to extend the flowering period 'plants with character', as Malcolm calls them, are also added. Typically these will include rose-pink *Lavatera cachemiriana* and pale yellow *Alcea rugosa*, both of which are short-lived perennials.

Thorough ground preparation is of the essence when renovating or planting a new wall border. Here are Malcolm's tips for success:

● Reduce the crown but leave a length of trunk to act as a

lever when removing large shrubs. Also dig out as many roots as possible to discourage the spread of honey fungus and other soil-borne diseases.

● If none exist already, secure a framework of horizontal wires to the wall, using tensioners and vine eyes to keep the wire taut. The distance between the wires should be about 30-45cm (12-18in), the lowest one being approximately 30cm (12in) above soil level.

● Refresh the border soil by digging in a 50:50 mix of imported loam and well-rotted farmyard manure.

● Plant your chosen wall shrubs and climbers, positioning them no closer than 30cm (12in) from the wall to avoid the rain shadow. Although pot-grown stock can be planted throughout the year, mid- to late spring is a favourable time to set out most plants, especially tender ones. Water generously for the first year until they are established.

● Apply a general fertiliser to the soil around their roots at the start of subsequent seasons and cover the soil with a 5-cm (2-in) thick layer of mulch; Malcolm swears by his own leafmould.

Tips

● To improve the quality of your plants, use a basic John Innes No.1 compost when pricking out or potting on, but adjust it to suit the needs of the plant in question. For example, add more grit for improved drainage when dealing with drought-loving species such as cistus or lavenders, but add more leafmould to increase the moisture-holding properties of the compost for abutilons, escallonias and vines. 'This is a useful tip I picked up when I worked at Kew Gardens,' says Malcolm.

● Use annual climbers like sweet peas, eccremocarpus, *Cobaea scandens* and *Tropaeolum canariensis* as temporary but colourful fillers until more permanent climbers become established in the border.

● In a northern garden such as Sizergh, winter protection for tender wall shrubs and climbers is now the norm. 'In the past I tended to risk the weather, but I am now starting to protect more plants, especially if they are new and have not become sufficiently established. In many cases it is not the cold which does the plants in, it is the wet,' he explains. Depending what the subjects are and where they are in the border, Malcolm either props over them a square frame of polythene sandwiched between sheep netting, or envelops them in a quilt of bracken, held between two sheets of chicken wire. The protection is put in place before Christmas and removed in March. 'Thereafter they take their chances,' he says.

Barrington Court

SOMERSET

Area: 4.5 ha (11 acres)
Soil: neutral/lime, loam
  over clay
Altitude: 20 m (65 ft)
Average rainfall: 762 mm (30 in)
Average winter climate: mild

When the National Trust took over management of Barrington Court in 1991, a detailed historical survey was undertaken so that a long-term management plan and conservation strategy for the garden could be drawn up. The overriding factor, as with all the Trust's properties, was to retain its unique qualities and atmosphere. It was decided, therefore, to restore the three elements introduced by Gertrude Jekyll – the Lily Garden, the Iris and Rose Garden and the Rose and Peony Garden – over a twenty-year period, while still respecting and maintaining the important contributions made by the long-term tenants of Barrington, the Lyle family.

Spearheading the restoration is Head Gardener Christine Brain, who came to the National Trust with the garden. Christine has been in charge at Barrington since 1978, the year she completed her diploma course at Cannington Horticultural College in Somerset. 'I love the peace and tranquillity here, and the fact that it is still gardened in a traditional manner. Although the Trust is very much aware of its history, there is still plenty of scope for experiment. As long as there is a challenge and the garden continues to move forward, it is always interesting,' she explains.

Climbers and wall plants at Barrington

Since much of the garden is made up of distinct walled enclosures or 'rooms', Barrington is generously endowed with vertical surfaces that support a wide range of climbers, wall shrubs and trained fruit trees. However, there are also a number of free-standing structures, like the brick pergola, parallel to the bustalls where veal calves were once reared, as well as the wooden archways in the Kitchen Garden, that are important features in themselves.

How plants are chosen depends on the individual areas they are to furnish. For instance, in the Kitchen Garden the deciding factor is often availability. Documentary evidence may point to a particular cultivar having grown there in the 1920s, but it may now have disappeared from cultivation, or been superseded by a better one. When this occurs, Christine sources a later cultivar, and if it happens to display any other attributes, such as increased resistance to pests and diseases, then so much the better.

A slightly different set of criteria comes into play with the three Jekyll gardens. Fortunately, the Trust was able to trace

Gertrude Jekyll's carefully drawn plans and plant lists to the University of Berkeley, California. These, together with old photographs and maps, form the basis of the restoration. First on the list, the Iris and Rose Garden, was completed in 1996. As a result twenty-four larch poles, clothed with the deep pink, thornless *Rosa* 'Zéphirine Drouhin', stand guard in the beds around the central sundial, while *Pyracantha coccinea* 'Lalandei', which has bright orange-red autumn berries, China roses and the pure white 'Dundee Rambler' rose festoon the surrounding walls. 'Where she did not make any suggestions, because there is now a wall instead of a hedge, we have borrowed her ideas from other gardens,' says Christine.

Such artistic licence will be granted throughout the restoration programme, for it is the overall effect, rather than strict historical accuracy, which is the crucial factor for the Trust. To stick rigidly to Miss Jekyll's original plans would be to deny the immense input of the Lyle family themselves. For the time being, the White Garden, which was planted in 1986 and presently occupies the site of the former Rose and Peony Garden, is to remain because it is immensely popular with visitors. For obvious reasons white-flowering climbers, such as *Wisteria floribunda* 'Alba', *Solanum jasminoides* 'Album' and white climbing 'Iceberg' roses, are the recurring theme there.

Wall-trained fruit trees at Barrington Court

Throughout spring, summer and autumn the large walled kitchen garden at Barrington Court is truly a sight to behold. Happily it is still wonderfully alive and bountiful, unlike the demise of many similar ones into car parks. Two crossing paths divide the area into four large quarters that produce orderly rows of vegetables, cut flowers and soft fruit for the restaurant that now occupies the Strode stable block.

Its surrounding Ham stone walls are home to an extensive range of espalier-, cordon- and fan-trained top fruit. 'The garden may look lovely and warm because it is enclosed, but the fruit can suffer quite badly from frost, which rolls down from the hills,' Christine reveals. For this reason siting the fruit trees against the most appropriate wall is vital for successful pollination and subsequent fruit set.

South-facing aspect: This is the warmest and sunniest wall, and should be reserved for less hardy fruit trees, such as peaches, nectarines, apricots and figs, although most fruit would thrive in this situation.

North-facing aspect: This is the coldest wall, but contrary to recommendations by most textbooks, Christine finds it very useful because it tends to delay the onset of flowering and as a result the plant often escapes late spring frosts. 'For example, damsons, gages and plums do surprisingly well on a north wall. Plant them anywhere else and they risk being frosted because they blossom that much earlier,' she says. Fruit generally ripens later on a north wall than it does in full sun. Morello cherries also thrive in this position.

East-facing aspect: This receives morning sun but is shaded in the afternoon. It is also open to cold easterly winds. Suitable fruits include late pears, apples, sweet and sour cherries.

West-facing aspect: This gets the afternoon sun and is generally wetter because it receives most rainfall. Suitable fruits include pears, apples, plums and gages.

Frost-tolerant cultivars

Although it should be noted that none are totally immune to frost, certain cultivars can tolerate it better than others. The selection is listed below in order of ripening, followed by a brief description of the fruit and its eating season:

Dessert apples (*Malus domestica*)

'Discovery' Small, crisp fruit with green-yellow and bright red skin. End of August to mid-September

'Worcester Pearmain' Small, sweet and perfumed fruit. September to October

'Greensleeves' Acid, crisp, greeny-yellow fruit. Middle of September to late November

'Ribston Pippin' Rich, sweet, crisp, striped fruit. November to January

'Sunset' Crisp and juicy, golden-yellow, flushed red fruit. November to December

'Suntan' 'Cox'-like flavour, but more acid. Golden-yellow, lightly striped skin. December to March. Flowers very late, therefore usually escapes frost

Culinary apples (*Malus domestica*)

'Lane's Prince Albert' Green-white, acid flesh, cooks well. Shiny, bright green, red-striped skin. January to March

'Edward VII' Acid, yellow, firm flesh, cooks dark red and transparent. December to April

'Annie Elizabeth' White, crisp flesh, excellent cooker. Pale yellow, red-striped skin. December to June

Pears (*Pyrus comunis*)

'Louise Bonne of Jersey' Sweet, white, melting flesh. Red-flushed, dotted, yellow-green fruits. October

'**Conference**' Sweet, firm, juicy flesh with dark olive skin. Mid-October to late November

'**Winter Nelis**' Sweet, perfumed, very juicy flesh. Dull green skin with dark brown russet. November to January

Culinary plums (*Prunus domestica*)

'**River's Early Prolific**' Small, oval, purple-blue fruit with golden flesh. Ripens late July to early August

'**Czar**' Oval, dark purple fruit with yellow-green flesh. Ripens early August

'**Marjorie's Seedling**' Large, oval, purple-blue fruit with yellow flesh. Ripens late September to early October

Acid cherries (*Prunus cerasus*)

'**Morello**' Reddish-black fruit with juicy, bitter-sweet flesh. Ripens August to September

Common pests and diseases of fruit at Barrington

The walled Kitchen Garden at Barrington Court may suit a wide range of fruit and vegetables, but it also provides a wonderful opportunity for pests and diseases to prosper. 'You name it, we get it,' jokes Christine. 'Although we are not organic, we try not to spray unless we have to.'

Some of the main problems at Barrington are given below, together with Christine's comments where appropriate:

● **Woolly aphid** The white woolly patches that develop on shoots and branches are actually the protective covering for these small brown aphids. 'We find that spraying with a product based on cresylic acid in December or January helps kill overwintering adults.'

● **Scab** A fungal disease predominately on apples, but also affecting pears, causing brown spots on the leaves, and lesions or swellings on branches and twigs. Worst in mild, damp weather. 'We tend not to spray for scab, but try to grow resistant varieties, such as 'Sunset'.'

● **Codling moth** Young grubs feed on and tunnel through the developing apples, or sometimes pears, from July to late August. Christine uses pheromone traps which attract and trap male moths by secreting a sex hormone. If they are put in place around the end of April, fewer males will be around to mate with the females, resulting in fewer eggs being laid.

● **Apple and plum sawfly** Cream-coloured larva, up to 15 mm (0·6 in) long, burrow into the developing fruit, which then falls prematurely, allowing the grubs to hibernate in the soil. 'We spray with a contact insecticide containing permethrin about a week after the petals have fallen.'

● **Red spider mite** Tiny brownish-red mites cause speckling of the leaves, and in severe cases may reduce the current crop as well as reducing the initiation of fruit buds for the following season. 'We spray with a systemic insecticide containing the ingredient heptenophos,' says Christine.

● **Peach leaf curl** Reddish blisters appear on the foliage which often falls prematurely. This fungal disease is spread by rain splash and is worst in cold, wet springs. 'We spray with a copper-based fungicide in late winter before the buds open and again in autumn after the leaves have fallen.'

● **Replant disease** If an old fruit tree is removed and replaced by a new one which never seems to become established, then suspect replant disease. The cause is thought to be a legacy of harmful micro-organisms left by the old tree that the newcomer cannot fend off. At Barrington peaches and nectarines are the main sufferers. 'We have tried digging out and replacing the old soil, as is often recommended, but this has not helped. And because they need the protection of a south-facing wall, we cannot plant them on a different site. At the moment we are growing them on in the middle of the Kitchen Garden with a view to moving them to their permanent homes when they are larger and more able to fend off the disease. We hope that will overcome the problem.'

Sweet peas at Barrington Court

Few annuals can compare to sweet peas for their colour, scent and long flowering period. They seem inexhaustible in their desire to please: the more you pick them, the more they reward you with fresh blooms for cutting. In fact, Christine considers picking them 'one of the perks of the job.'

About fourteen different cultivars are grown each year at Barrington, both in the kitchen garden, where single colours are planted on individual wigwams, and in the flower garden, where mixtures of soft blue, pink, mauve and cream are favoured. Not only do they provide height in the borders, they also make attractive floral focal points at the end of paths and walkways.

Bean poles and pea sticks, cut on a regular basis from nearby coppiced hazel woodland, provide the ideal means of support for sweet peas, as well as suiting the traditional theme of the garden. Rustic wigwams are then made by grouping strong, straight poles in a circle and tying them together at the top. Shorter, twiggy growths pushed in around the base form an initial foothold for twining tendrils.

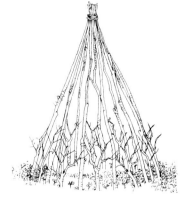

Sweet peas trained up a wigwam framework.

Growing sweet peas. Chitting the seed and removing the tips of seedlings to encourage bushy plants.

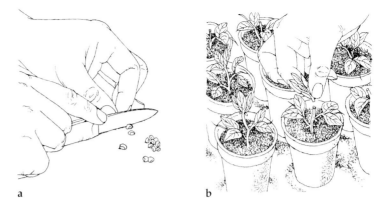

a   b

Christine offers the following tips when growing sweet peas:

● Sow seed in January for flowers from early June.

● To speed up intake of water and induce germination (a process known as scarification), chit the seed with a sharp knife by removing a small piece of seed coat opposite the eye (**a**). Soaking the seed in water has a similar effect, but is also more likely to cause the seed to rot.

● To minimise root disturbance, sow one or two seeds in individual 9cm (3.5in) pots. Push the seed into the compost to just cover it.

● Water, label and cover with a sheet of glass. Keep in a warm place, for instance an airing cupboard or heated greenhouse, until the seeds have germinated.

● As soon as shoots appear, remove the glass and place them in a light position.

● Grow them on and thin to the strongest seedling. Pinch out the growing tip after two true leaves have formed to encourage sideshoots and promote a bushy plant (**b**).

● Move outside to a coldframe in mid-February to grow on.

● Harden off and plant out into soil which has been enriched with well-rotted manure in March or April, depending on the weather. Space the plants about 20cm (8in) apart.

Planting for a brick pergola

Erected in 1981, the brick pergola at Barrington Court is a new addition, which replaces two large areas of bedding in front of the bustalls. As there was no historical precedent and therefore no planting plans to follow, the family had *carte blanche* over the climbers they could choose. 'We decided against roses because they were all round the garden already, and opted instead for a framework of vigorous specimens, such as honeysuckle, jasmine, golden hop and vines, to clothe the outside of the brick pillars and hang down from the wooden crossbeams above,' explains Christine.

For extra colour and impact, pairs of large-flowered clematis were planted on the inside of the pillars. These are pruned hard in early spring to strong pairs of buds about 15-30cm (6-12in) above soil level. New growth is then tied in around the brick piers and produces flowers at eye level from mid- to late summer. The cultivars used include:

C. **'Bees' Jubilee'** Deep pink flowers, fading with age, with a darker central band along each sepal. Prefers partial shade.

C. **'Hagley Hybrid'** Pinkish-mauve flowers, fading in full sun.

C. **'Jackmanii Superba'** Velvety, purple-blue flowers, fading in full sun.

C. **'Perle d'Azur'** Azure-blue flowers, recurved at the tips. Extremely floriferous.

C. **'Rouge Cardinal'** Velvety, crimson flowers. Prefers full sun.

The pergola is sited near a north-facing wall, so any underplanting must be tolerant of both shade and dry soil because it has to compete with the climbers overhead. *Euphorbia robbiae*, hellebores, Solomon's seal, epimedium, pulmonaria and alchemilla all thrive happily in these adverse conditions.

Plants for a productive and decorative walkway

A wooden, arched walkway makes a delightful feature in the kitchen garden, not simply because it defines one of the main paths, but also because it provides support for an inspired array of productive and decorative annual climbers. Each season it is planted with up to five different cultivars. In the past Christine has found the following very successful:

Ipomoea lobata **(syn.** *Mina lobata***)** A self-twining climber with racemes of narrow, tubular flowers that open crimson-red and fade to orange, yellow and white; flowers July to October; 1·2-1·8m (4-6ft) high.

Ipomoea purpurea **(common morning glory)** A twining annual climber with funnel-shaped purple-blue, pink or magenta flowers, and large heart-shaped leaves.

Runner bean: 'Painted Lady' is an old variety producing beautiful white and red blooms followed by tender, green pods; 'Scarlet Emperor' is a tried and tested favourite bearing scarlet flowers followed by long, slightly rough pods.

Climbing French bean 'Purple King' This bean has purple-tinged foliage and mauve flowers followed by attractive deep purple-black pods which turn bright green when cooked; harvest July to October; to 3m (10ft) tall.

Mixed climbing ornamental gourds A mixture of round and oval, smooth and warty, plain and variegated gourds for both indoor and outdoor decoration; harvest July to October; up to 2·4m (8ft) tall.

Vegetable spaghetti This annual bears long, oval, yellowish, marrow-like fruit. Boiled whole, they produce spaghetti-like flesh; harvest August to September; to 3m (10ft) tall.

Marrows and pumpkins The majority of cultivars form very large trailing plants with huge leaves, and with a little formative tying in, are as happy scaling heights as they are snaking along the ground. 'The only drawback is having to watch you don't hit your head on them!' laughs Christine. All are grown from seed, sown individually in pots under glass in April. Members of the marrow family germinate more successfully if the flattened seed is placed on its side just below the surface of the compost. When they are fully hardened off, they are planted out towards the end of May, about 30cm (12in) apart, with their own bamboo cane for support. Five or six plants, chosen more or less at random, span the distance between each wooden upright. In Christine's words, 'They jostle together and the bravest wins.'

Sowing marrow seed on its edge.

Overwintering tender plants

At Barrington Court Christine grows a number of plants she regards as tender for that part of the country. As a result they spend the winter months, from November to April, tucked up inside woven polypropylene fleece or netlon, the green shading material normally used in greenhouses. Straw is also packed around the base of the plant to protect its roots and crown. Figs, *Solanum jasminoides* 'Album' and *Trachelospermum asiaticum* are always cosseted in this way, as is the pink and white-tipped *Actinidia kolomikta*, which although hardy is easily damaged by late spring frosts. 'Many so-called tender plants require a certain amount of nursing when they are young, but as soon as they become established or too big to cover, they are better able to withstand the cold anyway,' she points out. That said, she does take plenty of cuttings as an insurance policy should any suffer an early demise.

Tips

● Ensure you train fruit from an early age, and do not be scared to make the first move. 'More often than not, people allow the tree to grow for about three or four years before deciding they want an espalier or fan-trained specimen. If they are not careful, growth runs away and they lose all hope of getting the tree back into shape.'

Winter protection for tender climbers.

● Allow the spring-flowering *Clematis armandii* to scramble over mature shrubs and trees. 'We find that if we try to train its stems neatly to the wall it just dies back, but if we leave it to grow through the nearby white-flowered *Chaenomeles speciosa* 'Moerloosei' it is far happier. When it threatens to suffocate its host, we simply cut it right back, as it seems to respond well to hard pruning.'

● Give established climbers a boost with a liberal sprinkling of slow-release fertiliser in spring. Most, but especially clematis, will also benefit from an application of sulphate of potash applied towards the end of summer. This helps firm up the wood for winter, as well as improving flower colour.

● Tie in the long, whippy stems of climbing roses as they form, and prune them as soon as possible in autumn when growth is still flexible.

Felbrigg Hall

NORFOLK

Area: 1 ha (2·75 acres)
Soil: neutral/light loam
Altitude: 61 m (200 ft)
Average rainfall: 635 mm (25 in)
Average winter climate: cold

In 1969 Felbrigg Hall was bequeathed to the National Trust by the last squire, Robert Windham Ketton-Cremer. Three years later, Ted Bullock, having gained valuable experience both at the Royal Horticultural Society's garden at Wisley in Surrey and also at Syon Park in Middlesex, was appointed Head Gardener to lead the restoration programme. 'When I first came to Felbrigg twenty-five years ago, the garden in general, and the wall-trained fruit in particular, was suffering from neglect. It has been tremendously satisfying to renovate it and clothe the walls with well-trained fruit trees once again,' says Ted enthusiastically.

Wall-trained fruit trees, climbers and wall plants at Felbrigg

Unlike many other properties acquired by the Trust, few records and plans about the garden at Felbrigg exist, therefore much of the restoration work has been based on detective work and conjecture. 'From the remnants of box hedging that we found, it was obvious where the paths and borders were, so we worked out a layout on that basis,' he explains. Although some of the old wall-trained fruit trees could be rescued, many more were so diseased or dilapidated that they had to be grubbed out. But what to put back in their place? An early stroke of good fortune steered the Trust in the present direction. 'When we started cultivating the soil, we kept coming across old fruit tree labels mainly dating back to 1879. It was decided to source these cultivars, along with other historic fruit varieties from the eighteenth and nineteenth centuries, and plant these along the most appropriate walls.'

Within the rectangular walled enclosure, the plot is further subdivided by two parallel walls running east to west. Not only does this create even more shelter from the wind, it also increases the vertical surface area on which to grow trained fruit, wall shrubs and climbers. Two of the three south-facing walls are given over to sun-loving fruit such as figs, dessert pears, apricots and peaches, while the third provides protection for a range of ceanothus and climbing roses. Conversely, their north-facing sides are less hospitable, but even they manage to support Morello cherries and the ornamental *Hydrangea anomala* subsp. *petiolaris*.

The bare walls are a feature in themselves. Rebuilt in 1824 with inferior bricks fired on the estate, they are comparatively soft and full of small stones. Whenever these drop out, the

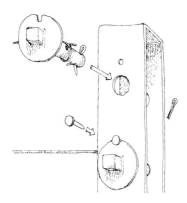

The wire tensioning device still used at Felbrigg.

wind scours the hole, giving an almost regular, pitted effect, rather like a sponge. Extra appeal is added by the wide assortment of nails driven into them over the years, with a few old horseshoe nails thrown in for good measure!

One of the south-facing walls has its original wire tensioning device still intact, which Ted continues to make use of today. A pair of iron stanchions, one with fixed bolts, the other with winding bolts, are clamped at opposite ends of the wall. A length of wire is then fastened to a fixed bolt at one end, and threaded through the hole in the shaft of the matching winding bolt at the other. This is then turned until the required tension is reached. When the notch in its circular disc lines up with the small hole in the stanchion, a nail or screw is passed through it to hold the bolt in position and prevent it slipping.

General principles for wall-trained fruit trees

● If planting on a site where fruit trees were previously grown, ensure you dig out a large hole; at Felbrigg this can be as much as 1·2m (4ft) square and 70cm (28in) deep. Fresh soil, enriched with well-rotted manure (except for figs, which should be treated to nothing richer than stony loam to avoid excessive leaf growth), is brought in using a tractor and trailer, to reduce the risk of replant disease, honey fungus or bacterial diseases. If transporting bulk loads poses a problem, Ted suggests using a soil sterilant on the existing ground instead. Plant the tree about 23–30cm (9–12in) out from the base of the wall to allow room for expansion and facilitate removal of sucker growth. Allow a distance of 4·8m (16ft) between each wall-trained tree.

● Help plants keep fighting fit to ward off diseases by watering, feeding and mulching generously. This advice is particularly pertinent to newly planted stock, but even old, established specimens will respond well to a little tender loving care.

● Most wall-trained fruit trees, especially apples and pears, are susceptible to mildew, which flourishes where air circulation is poor. 'We have had lots of problems in the past with mildew. I am sure the spores overwinter on the soft brickwork and the walls help keep in the disease,' says Ted. Good cultural methods will go a long way to limit possible outbreaks. Firstly, do not let other perennials, shrubs or climbers, such as clematis and roses, encroach upon the wall-trained tree, attractive though this may look; leave a gap of at least 90cm (3ft) in front of the trees to allow in light and air. Secondly, where apples and pears are grown, ensure you summer-prune, by removing the shoot tips in July, to open up congested growth. If mildew is still a problem, look for a fungicide containing carbendazim to control it.

● The rootstock onto which the fruit tree is grafted has the greatest influence on its ultimate size, but you should also take into account your soil type, as this too will have a bearing. 'Despite applying about sixty tons of well-rotted manure and garden compost on the borders each year at Felbrigg, the soil is still very light and free-draining. Even semi-dwarfing apple rootstocks have been unsuccessful here; they produce masses of blossom and fruit but rarely put on any new growth so are impossible to train. For that reason I favour more vigorous rootstocks, such as MM111. These will probably be too over-powering for most gardens, but I have found them the most successful on our poor soil,' he explains.

● Do not summer-prune any wall-trained fruit if it is under stress, for example if it is suffering from drought, nutrient deficiency or pest and disease attack. Your first priority should be to restore the tree to good health by watering, feeding and treating any problems.

Pears at Felbrigg

'Judging by the number of labels we found for pear varieties, it was obvious that they were a speciality here, so we decid-ed to stick with them,' explains Ted. Pears have much to commend them: they are as attractive as any Japanese cherry when in blossom; their malleable growth allows them to be trained as a fan, espalier, cordon, bush or standard; wall-trained trees can be especially productive; and given the right soil conditions, they also make long-lived specimens, so you can plant one knowing you will leave something behind for posterity. Their only disadvantage is that most tend to be self-sterile which means that more than one tree is needed for pollination and fruit set. Dessert pears are best grown on warm south- or west-facing walls, while culinary ones will tolerate a north-facing aspect.

Knowing when to harvest the fruit is an art in itself. It should not be left to ripen fully *in situ*. To ensure juicy, sweet dessert pears with that characteristic melting texture of butter, pick them while they are still firm, but when the fruit parts easily from the tree. Store them in a cool place but check them over regularly: their flesh has an uncanny habit of transforming itself into a disgusting brown mush almost before your very eyes. Culinary pears on the other hand, should be harvested as soon as the first fruits fall, even though some may not ripen in store until the following April.

Recommended dessert pear (*Pyrus communis*) cultivars at Felbrigg:

'Beurré Hardy' Large, russeted red fruit with juicy, white flesh. Harvest mid-September for use in October. Tree has fine autumn colour.

'Comte de Lamy' Small, conical, pale greenish-yellow fruit, with melting, white flesh. Harvest late September for use in October and November.

'Conference' Long, pale green fruit with yellowish flesh. Harvest from the end of September for use in October and November. Partially self-fertile.

'Doyenné du Comice' Large, golden fruit with creamy-white sweet flesh. Harvest from mid-October. Will keep for about a month in store.

Recommended culinary pears (*Pyrus communis*):

'Black Worcester' Large pear with brownish-red russeting. Will keep till April.

'Catillac' Very large, green pear. Harvest end of October. Ripens in April.

'Vicar of Winkfield' Very large, pale greenish-yellow fruit. Ripens in February.

Tackling overgrown figs

When Ted was first appointed Head Gardener, the figs, now neatly spread-eagled along the south-facing wall near the dovecote, came right out to the path, totally enveloping the 5m (15ft) wide border in front of them. Most of the branches, some as much as 20cm (8in) across, were cut back in one fell swoop. 'Although I wouldn't recommend this sort of treatment for most wall-trained fruit, figs respond very well to hard pruning, provided you water and mulch generously afterwards,' he says.

To keep them flat against the wall and to encourage fig formation, Ted prunes them twice a year. The fig is unusual among fruit trees in that three distinct stages of fruit development can be seen at one time. In their native habitat, where summers are longer and hotter than ours, the first to ripen are those on last year's wood, the next will be those on the current season's growth, then last to develop will be the embryonic fruit at the tips of the new shoots. But in our cool climate only this last group will ripen successfully. Ted's pruning regime is therefore directed at encouraging a plentiful supply of shoots and embryo figs, which, if successfully overwintered, should develop and ripen the following August or September:

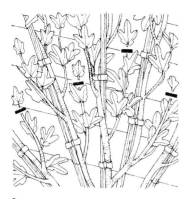

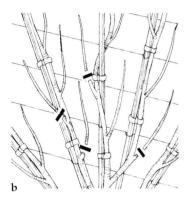

Pruning figs in summer (**a**) and winter (**b**).

A vine pruned for winter, showing the supporting quadripod (**a**).
Summer pruning for vines (**b**).

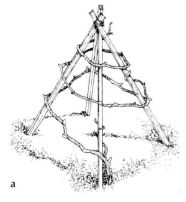

● In June remove the tips from about half the laterals, leaving about five or six leaves. As the lower buds break and shoots develop, tie them in (**a**).

● From October to mid-November prune back to 2·5cm (1 in) half the shoots that carried fruits. This encourages new growth from the base the following spring. Tie in the remaining shoots, about 23-30cm (9-12in) apart. Cut out any growth in between to keep the framework open (**b**).

Vines for height

The range of structures that can be dreamt up to support climbers is almost as numerous as the plants that can be selected to clothe them. At Felbrigg six ingenious timber wigwams, known as 'quadripods', are used along the centre of a border. Enveloped with outdoor vines, which are particularly appropriate in a walled kitchen garden, they are primarily a decorative feature to add height among shrub roses, but they also produce a reasonable crop of fruit when summers are hot. 'Müller Thurgau' and 'Seyval Blanc' bear sweet white grapes, while 'Brant' and 'Wrotham Pinot' have small, sharply-flavoured, black fruit but very ornamental foliage.

The wigwams are made up of four tanalised timber posts, 2·7m (9ft) long by 3·8cm (1·5in) square, which are driven into the soil at an angle until about 2m (6·5ft) remains above ground. The posts should be about 1·5m (5ft) apart each way at the bottom. Each quadripod supports just one vine, the leading shoot of which is wound round the outside of the stakes and tied in as it grows. To keep the grape within bounds, pruning is carried out twice a year:

● In January the laterals are cut right back to two buds (**a**).

● In July lateral growth is stopped at two leaves beyond the last bunch of grapes. For the best fruit a maximum of two bunches is allowed for each lateral, and any sub-laterals are pinched out to one leaf (**b**).

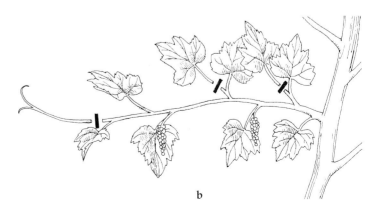

Wall-trained ceanothus

Ceanothus, or California lilac, do exceptionally well at Felbrigg. The garden's free-draining soil coupled with a sheltered position on one of the south-facing walls do much to ensure rapid growth and an unparalleled display of sky-blue flowers, often produced in such profusion that the foliage almost disappears beneath a blue haze. Evergreen species are said to be more tender than deciduous ones, so these in particular benefit from the protection afforded by a sunny wall. In this position they will usually attain greater heights than those grown as free-standing border shrubs. Those at Felbrigg include:

C. **'A.T. Johnson'** Vigorous, bushy evergreen with light green foliage and rich blue flowers in late spring and again from late summer to autumn. Grows to 3 m (10ft).

C. **'Autumnal Blue'** Upright evergreen with glossy, bright green foliage and sky-blue flowers from late summer to autumn. Grows to 3 m (10ft).

C. **'Burkwoodii'** Bushy and compact evergreen with glossy, dark green foliage and bright blue flowers from late summer to autumn. Grows to 1·8–3 m (6–10ft).

C. dentatus Densely branched evergreen with rigid shoots and small, dark green leaves. Dark blue flowers are produced in late spring. Grows to 3 m (10ft).

C. **'Gloire de Versailles'** Bushy, deciduous shrub with pale blue flowers that appear from mid-summer to autumn. Grows to 1·8–2·4 m (6–8ft) tall.

C. impressus Cascading evergreen with deeply veined, dark green leaves and dark blue flowers from mid- to late spring. Particularly good on a wall. Grows to 3 m (10ft).

C. **'Southmead'** Compact, bushy evergreen with dark green leaves and rich blue flowers in late spring and early summer. Grows to 3 m (10ft)

How and when ceanothus are pruned at Felbrigg depends on the age of wood which bears the flowers:

● Deciduous species which flower on the current season's growth in late summer are cut back to a permanent framework in mid-spring (**a**).

● Evergreen species which flower on growth made in the previous season are pruned immediately after they have finished flowering, removing any shoots that are growing away from the wall, and pruning back all remaining growth by about a third if it is not needed to fill gaps in the permanent framework (**b**).

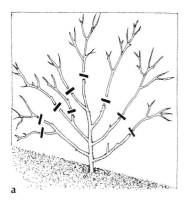

a

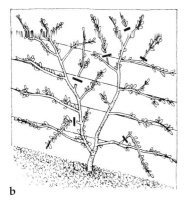

b

Pruning deciduous (**a**) and evergreen (**b**) ceanothus.

Tips

● July is the safest time to work on stone fruits such as plums, cherries, peaches and apricots; any pruning cuts made in winter leave trees open to a fatal disease known as silver leaf. Ted finds the finger and thumb method the most efficient way of pruning young sideshoots. Pinching them back while the growth is still soft is not only quicker than using secateurs, but it also reduces the likelihood of disease since pruning wounds are smaller.

● Avoid tip-bearing cultivars when choosing apples for wall training. To ensure a good coverage of fruit all over the tree, always go for spur-bearers.

● Although using wound paint is no longer advocated in most horticultural circles, Ted is the first to sing its praises. 'When I first came here, I had to remove large branches from much of the wall-trained fruit. To prevent disease spores entering the tree, I immediately applied a wound paint and then nailed roofing felt over the cut. This method was even successful on cherries which are known to be difficult.'

● Avoid tarred twine for tying in young shoots, use soft string or fillis instead. 'I have a feeling that the tar in the string reacts with sunlight. The young growth on peaches and apricots seems to be particularly susceptible,' says Ted.

● Do not buy partly trained fan or espalier fruit trees in a bid to save yourself time: few will have been correctly pruned in the early years. If you start with a maiden whip (a one-year-old tree with a single stem), and follow the advice laid out in a fruit manual, you are more or less assured of success, and you will have the satisfaction of knowing your creation is of your own making.

Westbury Court Garden

GLOUCESTERSHIRE

Area: 2ha (5 acres)
Soil: alkaline/alluvial silt, clay
Altitude: 6m (20ft)
Average rainfall: 686mm (27in)
Average winter climate:
   moderate

Gardener-in-Charge Ken Vaughan has been involved at West-bury Court almost as long as the Trust. 'Before I came here in 1970, I had read about this extraordinary garden that had lain derelict for so long. Seeing through the restoration project from start to finish has been an enjoyable and rewarding experience.'

Restoration involved clearing, dredging and relining the walls of the seventeenth-century canals, replanting hedges, repairing the gazebo and totally rebuilding the Dutch-style pavilion at the head of the Long Canal. The long brick wall that runs the entire length of the drive was also reconstructed.

Fortunately, the Trust could draw on a wealth of documentary evidence to help in this work. An account book, held in the Gloucestershire Records Office, helped to date much of the surviving work as well as give the exact numbers and kinds of plants Maynard Colchester purchased for the beds and borders. Furthermore, a bird's-eye view of Westbury, engraved by Johannes Kip around 1707, provided a vital pictorial record of the original layout.

Wall-trained fruit trees, climbers and wall plants at Westbury

An orderly line of wall-trained apple, pear and plum trees are planted along the south-east face of the long brick wall rebuilt during the restoration of the garden. Evocative-sounding varieties such as 'Lemon Pippin' (apple), 'Catshead' (apple), 'Bellisime d'Hiver' (pear), 'Gross Reine Claude' (plum) may not be familiar to most garden visitors today, but Maynard Colchester would have known them, for they were all in cultivation before 1700. Brogdale Horticultural Trust in Kent, holder of the largest National Collection of tree fruits in the country, provided much of the grafting material for these unusual old cultivars.

The south-west facing wall, that runs parallel to the main road into the village of Westbury, is home to a number of tender wall shrubs and climbers. The bay tree, *Laurus nobilis*, and passion flower, *Passiflora caerulea*, are now common sights in our gardens today but less well known is *Paliurus spina-christi*, the wickedly thorny, glossy-leaved shrub with small yellow flowers, from which Christ's 'crown of thorns' was said to have been made. Similarly unfamiliar is the chaste tree, *Vitex agnus-castus*, with its purple-blue flower spikes and attractive, widely spread, finger-like foliage. Ken fan-trains both shrubs against the wall.

The small walled garden by the gazebo, which was developed later, also boasts its share of climbers, as well as a collection of nineteenth-century shrub roses. A matrix of crossing gravel paths divides this enclosed space into rectangular borders edged with dwarf box, while oak posts, surmounted by simple, flattened metal arches provide height and vertical interest above the central path. From early to late summer three kinds of honeysuckle, *Lonicera periclymenum*, *L. periclymenum* 'Belgica' and *L. caprifolium* furnish these arches with intoxicating white, yellow or pink-flushed flowers which are eclipsed by orange-red or scarlet berries later in the year. Similarly constructed corner arbours with built-in seats support a veil of vines and the light pink rambler *Rosa* 'Adélaïde d'Orléans'.

Coping with problem soil

With its high water-table, the low-lying land at Westbury Court regularly succumbs to flooding. These natural conditions are tailor-made for moisture-lovers and bog plants that adore dangling their toes in water, but are far less conducive to the fruit trees which were historically grown in the garden. Peaches and apricots languish in the soil, and some of the plums are far from happy. At the start of the restoration, the National Trust had one deep drain installed, but it soon became evident that this was not enough. Secondary drainage channels were therefore put in where appropriate but even they have not proved entirely effective.

Ken has found the conditions a constant challenge. 'When I first arrived the soil was in a shocking state. It is termed alluvial silt which tends to be very sticky and difficult to work in winter but dries out like concrete in summer.' Over the years several hundred tons of topsoil have been imported to make up the levels where trees and hedges had to be grubbed out, and this has made an appreciable difference. Ken also ensures he adds a 15cm (6in) layer of gravel at the bottom of planting holes, particularly in parts of the garden which are most at risk from flooding.

Such an area is the long rectangular tongue of ground between the two canals that used to be Maynard Colchester's vegetable garden. As part of the restoration project the Trust replanted the plum trees which originally surrounded it, but curiously many failed to flourish. 'On digging them all up, we discovered a layer of solid, impermeable clay about 60cm (2ft) below the surface of the soil. Where the clay was undisturbed, the trees were quite happy, where it had been broken up by cultivation, it had created a sump filled with water that was unable to drain away. It was on these spots that the trees died,' he explains. The plums have since been replaced by shallow-rooting box spires, all of which are thriving.

How to grow an espaliered apple or pear tree

If you have never grown an espaliered tree before, try starting on a pear tree as they have much to commend them to the beginner. 'Pears have got more pliable, biddable stems than apples. They are less prone to disease, and if you make a mistake they will almost grow a new shoot for you overnight,' says Ken enthusiastically.

● To support the espalier, install a system of parallel horizontal wires about 45-60cm (18-24in) apart.

● Begin with a one-year-old 'maiden whip' which has a clear, upright stem without lateral branches. For a pear espalier with two or three tiers, ensure the maiden is grafted onto 'Quince C' rootstock; for further tiers go for the more vigorous 'Quince A' rootstock.

● In winter plant the maiden whip about 15-23cm (6-9in) away from the base of the wall or fence. Cut the stem back to a good bud 2·5cm (1in) below the first wire. Ensure there are two healthy buds just below it, pointing in opposite directions to form the framework for the lowest tier.

● In summer train the three main shoots to three bamboo canes tied to the wires. The leader should be tied in vertically, while the two arms should be spread out at an angle of 45° to help prevent any check in their growth during the first year (**a**).

● During the second winter carefully lower the canes and tie them in to the horizontal wires. At the same time prune the new leader to a good bud 2·5cm (1in) below the next wire, again ensuring there are two healthy buds below it facing in opposite directions to form the second tier (**b**).

● During the second summer, tie in the next three shoots as before. In addition cut back the laterals on the first horizontal tier to three or four leaves. This will begin the process known as spur formation which will bear the fruit (**c**).

● During the third winter lower the bamboo canes to a horizontal position, and prune back the leader as before (**d**).

● Continue this method of alternate summer and winter pruning and tying in until the tiered skeleton is formed (**e**).

● Thereafter general pruning is confined to the summer months, usually around July, which involves cutting back new laterals from the main stem to three leaves above the basal cluster (the lowest circle of leaves on a shoot). Any new growth arising from existing sideshoots and spurs should be reduced to just one leaf above the basal cluster.

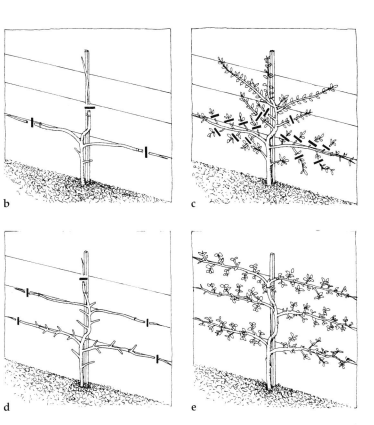

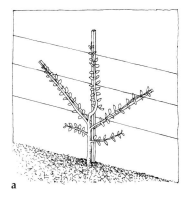

Growing an espaliered fruit tree.

Recommended apple and pear cultivars at Westbury

After years of being offered the usual selection of apples and pears both in supermarkets and garden centres, it is gratifying to see some of our oldest cultivars enjoying something of a revival. The fact that the National Collection at Brogdale grows about 2,200 cultivars of *Malus* alone gives some indication of our enormous apple heritage. Granted, not all will be garden worthy, for instance if they are overly susceptible to pests and diseases, but many will hold their own in terms of flavour and appearance.

At Westbury Ken grows approximately twenty historic cultivars of apples and pears, most of which date back to before 1700. The ones most readily available at specialist fruit nurseries include the following:

Apples (*Malus domestica*)

'Ashmead's Kernel' (early eighteenth century) Crisp and juicy, superior in flavour to 'Cox'. Grey-brown russet appearance. Moderate yield and vigour. Harvested in October, will keep as late as March in cold storage.

'Calville Blanc d'Hiver' (1598) A famous French winter cultivar. Large, strongly scented dessert apple with a pink cheek. Unfortunately this cultivar is not always hardy in cold districts. Harvested in late October, it will ripen in December and January and keep till March.

'Catshead' (mid-seventeenth century) Extremely large cooking apple with pale yellow skin. Harvested in October, will keep till January.

'Court Pendu Plat' (1613) Very old apple, said to have been grown since Roman times. Small, flattish, round fruit with dull yellow, red-flushed skin. Flowers very late therefore not prone to frost. Also scab resistant. Harvested in late October, will keep as late as April.

'Devonshire Quarrenden' (1678) Crisp and juicy with a distinctive flavour. Shining dessert apple with dark crimson skin. Harvest and eat August to September.

'Nonpareil' (mid-sixteenth century) Small, dull but richly flavoured dessert apple. Harvested late October, will ripen in December and January.

'Wyken Pippin' (1700) Small, flattened fruit with delicious flavour and dull, greenish-yellow skin. Harvested mid-October, will keep to February.

Pears (*Pyrus communis*)

'Catillac' (1665) Very large, green cooking pear, particularly good for stewing, remaining hard until April. Resistant to scab. Makes a spreading tree with broad leaves and large flowers unlike any other pear.

'Black Worcester' (sixteenth century) Large culinary pear, with brownish-red russeting, unpalatable until cooked. Will keep till April.

'Jargonelle' (seventeenth century) Small, greenish-yellow tapering fruit, cropping freely once established. Resistant to scab. Harvest when still green as soon as they part from the tree, and store in a cool room until ripe.

Tips

● To stimulate the growth of dormant buds on trained forms of fruit trees, Ken uses a process known as 'notching,' which involves removing a narrow, crescent-shaped strip of bark just above a bud. This creates a build-up of pressure in the flow of sap up the stem and encourages the dormant bud to spring into life. 'I have found this to be as effective on old specimens as young ones, the only difference is that the larger the operation, the cruder the tools. Instead of a penknife, you end up using a saw, hammer and chisel. But it works!'

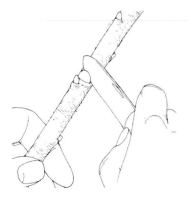

Notching to stimulate the growth of dormant buds.

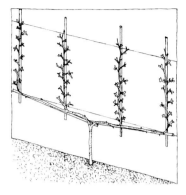

A multiple cordon: an attractive and productive method of training fruit trees.

● Once you get the hang of training fruit trees, you can let your imagination run riot and experiment with all manner of decorative shapes. Ken has grown so many trained trees that he can almost do espaliers in his sleep, but he has also had great success with multiple cordons, which not only look attractive but are highly productive as well.

● The ultimate size of most fruit trees is governed largely by the rootstocks onto which they are grafted. Therefore it is vital to choose the most appropriate one for your needs. You will be locked in constant battle with an espaliered apple tree which has been grafted onto a vigorous rootstock, if you expect it to stay within the confines of a 1·8-m (6-ft) high wall.

● It is not always necessary to entirely replace a wooden vertical post that has rotted off in the soil, thereby disturbing its mantle of climbing plants in the process. Drive a metal post support into the ground next to it, saw off the timber column at ground level and insert it into the neck of the metal sleeve.

● In theory you need only keep four chemicals to combat pests and diseases on most fruit trees (and many ornamentals too): a contact and systemic insecticide, together with a contact and systemic fungicide. Spraying them on alternate occasions to control the relevant problem will reduce the likelihood of resistant strains developing.

Erddig

CLWYD

Area: 5·2ha (13 acres)
Soil: slightly acid/loam
  and clay
Altitude: 61m (200ft)
Average rainfall: 889mm (35in)
Average winter climate:
  moderate

Glyn Smith has been Head Gardener at Erddig for thirteen years. Before coming here in 1984, he worked as Garden Supervisor of the Decorative Department at the Royal Botanic Gardens, Kew, which stood him in good stead for his present job. 'One of the most satisfying things about working here is seeing visitors enjoying the garden and hearing their comments about it,' says Glyn. 'It would also be nice to enjoy a peach or apricot every now and then,' he adds jokingly, referring to the fact that in all his years at Erddig he has gathered but a handful of these fruits because squirrels, birds and two-legged predators always seem to beat him to it!

Wall-trained fruit trees and climbers at Erddig

The garden at Erddig is strongly influenced by the formal Dutch style of the late seventeenth century. Unlike the pomp and grandeur of formal French and Italian layouts, Dutch gardens were usually simpler and more intimate in scale with a greater emphasis on flowers, as well as the production of more useful plants such as herbs, vegetables and fruit.

Thomas Badeslade's engraving of 1739 revealed that the extensive 2·4m (8ft) high wall around the main garden provided support for trained fruit trees, while original lists made in 1718 and 1725 indicated more precisely which cultivars were actually grown. The Trust tracked down and put back as many as possible. These were principally fan-trained stone fruits such as plums, peaches and apricots, as well as vines and espaliered pears. Apples were conspicuously absent from the list, suggesting that they made up the blocks of planting in the orchard. 'Even though they were not originally grown there, we have added historic varieties of espaliered apples to the walls. As they can be tackled in winter, we find apples and pears suit our working practices better than the stone fruit, which has to be pruned in summer, when we simply do not have the time or the staff to give them the attention they require,' explains Glyn.

To extend colour and interest throughout the visiting season the wall-trained fruit has been interplanted with a range of climbing plants such as clematis, solanum, honeysuckle and jasmine, but their often rampant growth is never allowed to encroach upon the branches of the adjacent fruit trees. Those, like *Clematis viticella* or sweet peas, which are cut down annually, are provided with a pillar of brushwood. This not only helps contain growth, it also speeds up winter pruning, for after being given the chop, the whole lot, twiggy plant supports and all, can be tossed into the back of a trailer in one go.

Erddig is also home to one of the National Collections of *Hedera* (ivy) cultivars, held for the National Council for the Conservation of Plants and Gardens (NCCPG). In the main these are to be found on the shaded north-facing wall of the formal garden, on the walls around the car park which was formerly the old kitchen garden, as well as on some of the outbuildings. At the last count the collection totalled around 180, but Glyn is constantly adding to it.

The ivy collection

Quite why the property was chosen to house the ivy collection is a mystery to Glyn, but the fact that it boasts such an extensive surface area of walls must have played some part. 'A trial of ivies was held by the Royal Horticultural Society at Wisley in 1977 to sort out their nomenclature and potential as garden plants. When it came to an end two years later, it was hoped that the clones in the trial might be kept together to form the basis of a National Collection. Eventually this was made possible by the Trust's offer to plant some of that material here at Erddig,' he says. They were initially planted following the original Wisley order, but more recently a decision was taken to rearrange them in a more meaningful way. With this in mind, they are being re-propagated where necessary, and different cultivars of the same species are being grouped together so that comparisons can be drawn more easily.

As well as conserving ivies, one of the purposes of the collection is to show their different patterns of growth. 'We are generally told that they show two distinct stages – the juvenile climbing stage and the adult non-clinging phase – but I would argue that very often there can be more than that. As a ground-cover, ivies sometimes throw out different foliage to when they first climb. Once they start to grow vertically, their self-clinging stems can produce two distinct leaf types. In the final stage when they reach the top of their support, the juvenile, lobed foliage is replaced by much more bushy growth with more rounded leaves and spherical black or sometimes yellowish fruits in the case of the poet's ivy. Where possible, I want to show the whole life story of the plant in one picture,' Glyn enthuses.

'Most people do not realise how their prized houseplant will respond when let loose in the garden. One of the interests of the collection is that it shows how ivies produce uncharacteristic shoots.' For example, *Hedera* 'Professor Friedrich Tobler' has small, deeply lobed, green leaves when grown in a pot, but unleash it outside where it can scale dizzy heights, and you get much larger, digitate foliage which looks almost exactly the same as a cultivar known as *H.*'Königers Auslese'.

When they are grown *en masse*, it is far easier to compare the cultivars and note any attributes as well as drawbacks the plant may have. *H.*'Goldheart', for instance, tends to lose its central yellow splash when grown as a groundcover, but on a sunny wall its attractive foliage is unsurpassed. *H.*'Shamrock', the dark green, clover-leaf ivy, is slow to establish on walls and is probably best used for topiary or in a hanging basket. The cream and grey variegated *H.*'Anne Marie' is consistent in her growth, while *H.*'Brokamp', which should have unlobed green foliage is prone to revert to a more digitate form.

Ivy cultivation

As a rule, ivies rarely require bribing or cajoling into perform-ing well because they are a very easy, unfussy group of plants. Although they withstand a range of conditions, they do best given moist, free-draining, slightly alkaline soil. Green-leaved cultivars tend to be hardier and more tolerant of shade than their showy, variegated cousins which require more light and some shelter from the wind.

Other than cutting them back in winter where they have ventured too far from the wall, Glyn finds the ivies at Erddig very undemanding. 'They regenerate readily from old wood and can be pruned back hard if necessary to restrict height and spread,' recommends Glyn. He also points out that ivies seldom cause damage if walls are sound, but the weight of the plant can peel away loose or soft mortar, and repointing may be required. 'It is advisable to remove shoots near slates, gutters and drainpipes because ivy may cause them to lift as it matures and thickens,' he says.

Propagation of ivies

To obtain plants with a trailing or climbing habit, take cuttings of juvenile growth between late spring and early autumn. To achieve a flowering and fruiting ivy shrub, take cuttings of the adult stage in spring or summer. The latter are more difficult to propagate, often taking up to six months to form roots, but Glyn has been successful using the following method:

● Select a healthy, non-flowering shoot, 5–15cm (2–6in) long, from the parent plant.

● Remove the leaves from the bottom half of the shoot, and cut the remaining ones in half to reduce water loss.

● Trim the cutting just below a node and dip the base in hormone rooting powder.

- Insert the cutting into a pot containing cutting compost made up of 50:50 sharp sand to peat substitute.
- Water with a fine mist spray, place in a propagator and position in a light, warm spot to form roots.

Recommended cultivars for the garden

There are over 300 known cultivars of *Hedera*, but most garden centres and nurseries will stock just a handful of the most popular. For the greatest choice you will have to visit or order from a specialist ivy grower such as Fibrex Nurseries, of Stratford-upon-Avon, Warwickshire.

From his experience of ivies, Glyn recommends the following cultivars for the garden:

'Angularis Aurea' Shallowly lobed, glossy, mid-green leaves which become marbled and variegated with yellow, particularly if grown in sun. Ideal for a wall. Grows to 5m (15ft).

'Atropurpurea' Large, pointed, five-lobed, dark green foliage, turning deep purple in cold weather. Good on a high wall. Grows to 8m (25ft).

'Buttercup' Large, five-lobed leaves that are lime-green in shade but bright yellow in full sun. Good on a wall. Grows to 1·8m (6ft).

'Congesta' Non-climbing ivy, forming a pert bush with small, three-lobed, dark green leaves up stiffly erect stems. Ideal for a rock garden. 45cm (18in) high.

'Glacier' Small, three- to five-lobed, grey-green leaves with cream and grey variegation. Good all-rounder for walls, ground cover, or in pots both inside and outside. Grows to 1·8m (6ft).

'Golden Ingot' Small, pointed, three- to five-lobed, green leaves with broad yellow margins. Good in pots or on a low wall. Grows to 1m (3ft).

'Green Ripple' Jaggedly lobed, mid-green leaves, the central lobe being long and tapering. Good on a wall. Grows to 1·8m (6ft).

'Lalla Rookh' Medium-sized, irregularly toothed, five-lobed, light green leaves, cut almost to the central veins. Its trailing habit makes it particularly useful for hanging baskets. Grows to 1m (3ft).

'Mrs. Pollock' Medium-sized, five- to seven-lobed, mid-green leaves, suffused with yellow as it ages, but totally green when young. Good on a high wall. Grows to 3m (10ft).

'Pedata' (bird's foot ivy) Medium-sized, five-lobed, grey-green leaves, the elongated central lobe and backward-pointing lateral lobes resembling the imprint of a bird's claw. Ideal for a high wall. Grows to 4m (12ft).

H. hibernica '**Deltoidea**' (**sweetheart ivy**) Large, rounded, or very shallowly three-lobed, dark green leaves, the basal lobes of which overlap creating a heart-shaped appearance. Slow-growing but will eventually reach 5m (15ft).

Growing a fan-trained Morello cherry

Glyn may not have the time or the manpower to lavish attention on the majority of stone fruit in the garden, but when it comes to the four fan-trained Morello cherries that hug a length of the high, north-facing, brick wall, no expense is spared. Their neatly trained framework of radiating ribs is as exemplary as any you would find in a pruning manual. 'The art of pruning anything is all about planning and having a feel for the plant,' he says. Here are his tips for success:

● Plant a young feathered tree about 23cm (9in) away from the wall in autumn or winter.

● In February select two well-placed laterals to form the main arms, one on either side, and prune out the leader just above the higher one. Shorten each lateral to about 38cm (15in), and tie each one to a bamboo cane, attached at an angle of 40° to the horizontal wires on the wall (**a**).

● In summer, select four well-placed shoots on each arm to form the main ribs, and tie these to bamboo canes set at the desired angle. Prune back all other shoots to one leaf (**b**).

● The following February, shorten the main ribs by about a quarter to encourage further branching (**c**).

● During the second summer, tie in well-placed sideshoots as they develop, allowing shoots to grow every 10cm (4in), and adding canes where necessary to create an even framework. Where growth is crowded, cut back stems to four leaves above the basal cluster. In late summer pinch out the growing tips when the selected laterals have made 45cm (18in) of new growth. These will bear fruit the following year (**d**).

● Acid cherries fruit mainly on growth made during the previous season, so pruning the established fan-trained tree favours these one-year-old shoots. With this in mind, in early summer thin out new shoots to about 10cm (4in) apart and tie them in (**e**).

● In late August, after harvesting the cherries, cut out the laterals that carried the fruit, pruning them back to the young replacement shoots lower down. Tie these in evenly to fill the framework, as they will be the shoots that will bear fruit the following summer (**f**).

Fan-training a Morello cherry tree.

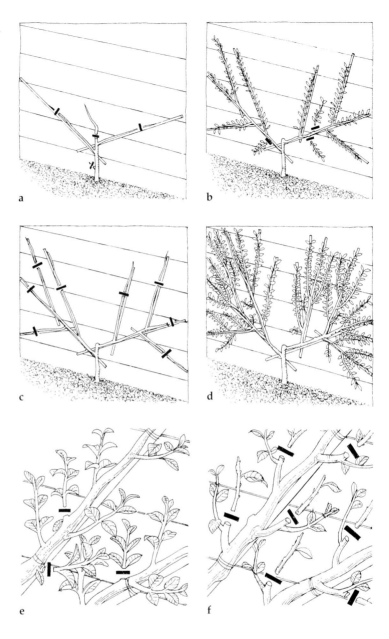

Rose and clematis pillars

At Erddig a Victorian-style flower garden has been recreated following an earlier design. Here a series of rustic poles, each one planted with the pink rambler rose 'Dorothy Perkins' and purple *Clematis* 'Jackmanii', tower above low rope swags, festooned by yet more roses.

To achieve such a billowing, but balanced effect, skilful pruning is required if the clematis is not to completely smother its partner. In late summer after both have finished flowering, Glyn removes all but four of the newest, lowest stems from the rose, and prunes back the clematis to about 60cm (24in) above the ground. In spring just four clematis shoots are allowed to grow, the rest are snapped off. 'This may sound ruthless, but it still produces a fine display,' assures Glyn. It is important to tie in the stems of both climbers throughout the season to ensure a neat outline. 'I have also driven in a long nail at the end of each post, to which I secure the topmost growth, otherwise the whole lot slips down, rather like Nora Batty's stockings!' he laughs.

Glyn admits it is not an easy combination to manage. 'If I were planting up rustic posts in my own garden, I would choose less vigorous plants that work better together. Climbing roses such as white *R*. 'Climbing Iceberg', or pink and white *R*. 'Handel', are more than worthy alternatives as they are repeat flowering and neater in their growth than rambler roses. Many of the *Clematis viticella* cultivars are also far less overwhelming than the clematis used here.'

Tips

● When choosing plants for walls and fences, do not restrict yourself to conventional climbers alone. Remember many hardy shrubs, more usually seen as free-standing specimens in the border, lend themselves to being pruned and trained more formally against a vertical structure, as a fan or in horizontal tiers. Those suitable for walls include chaenomeles, *Cotoneaster horizontalis*, *Forsythia suspensa* and pyracantha. Do not be afraid to experiment.

● The uses for ivy in the garden are endless. As well as clothing walls or hugging the soil as groundcover, you can grow ivy along ugly fences and clip the resulting growth as you would any other hedge, an effect sometimes referred to as a 'fedge'. The impatient gardener may like to know that you can train it over wire frames to achieve more or less instant topiary shapes. This certainly beats waiting years for more traditional box or yew specimens to reach maturity. Small-leaved cultivars can even be trained as trailing standards. To do this, pot up a single-stemmed cutting and tie it to a cane. Remove all sideshoots as it grows and nip out the leader when it has reached the desired height. Pinch out the tips of the subsequent shoots to create a bushy head and a cascade of trailing growth.

Plant Directory

Wall plants, climbers and fruit for a sunny aspect

Abutilon megapotamicum A semi-evergreen shrub with arching shoots and dangling, bell-shaped flowers, comprising of yellow or apricot petals protruding from red calyces, during summer and autumn. Grows to 1·8m (6ft). *A. × suntense* is much larger altogether, growing to 4m (12ft), with saucer-shaped, white to violet-blue blooms. If growing flat against a wall, cut back to within two to four buds of the framework in early spring.

Actinidia kolomikta A deciduous, twining climber with olive-green leaves that look as though they have been half dipped in white and pink paint. Grows to 5m (15ft) or more. In early spring shorten growth to one-third or half its length, pruning to a healthy bud.

Billardiera longiflora A wiry-stemmed, half-hardy evergreen climber with small, tubular, pale greeny-yellow flowers, followed by rounded, deep purple fruits. Requires neutral to acid humus-rich soil. Grows to 1·8-3m (6-10ft). Trim after flowering to fit available space.

Campsis radicans A vigorous, deciduous climber with attractive pinnate foliage and long, trumpet-shaped, scarlet flowers from late summer to autumn (above). Self-clinging once established. Grows to 4m (12ft) or more. *C. × tagliabuana* 'Madame Galen' is very reliable and vigorous with salmon-red flowers, but it does require support. In early spring spur-prune sideshoots to within three or four buds of the framework. Overgrown specimens respond well to hard pruning.

Ceanothus See page 70

Clematis An indispensable genus of some ever-green, but mostly deciduous climbers. Their flowers may be flat, cupped or bell-shaped, and they are sometimes followed by fluffy seedheads. All clematis prefer to have their roots in shade and their top growth in sun. Recommended cultivars for spring include: *C. alpina* 'Frances Rivis' (nodding blue bells; to 3m (10ft) tall); *C. macropetala* 'Markham's Pink' (nodding, semi-double, clear pink flowers; to 3m (10ft) tall); *C. montana* 'Elizabeth' (fragrant, pale pink flowers; purple-flushed foliage; to 7m (22ft) tall); and *C. montana* f. *grandiflora* (white flowers with cream anthers; to 10m (30ft) tall).

Next to bloom are the large-flowered hybrid clematis, the best of which include: 'Carnaby' (deep-pink, white-edged flowers, fading in full sun; to 2·4m (8ft) tall); 'Countess of Lovelace' (double, lavender-blue flowers; to 1·8m (6ft) tall); 'Miss Bateman' (white flowers with purple stamens; to 2·4m (8ft) tall); 'Niobe' (rich deep red flowers with yellow anthers; to 3m (10ft) tall); and 'The President' (rich purple flowers with silver undersides; bronze foliage when young; to 3m (10ft) tall).

July to September-flowering clematis include: 'Abundance' (open bell-shaped, wine-red flowers; to 3m (10ft) tall); 'Alba Luxurians' (open bell-shaped, white flowers, tipped with green; to 4m (12ft) tall); 'Etoile Violette' (nodding, saucer-shaped, violet-purple flowers; to 5m (15ft) tall); 'Madame Julia Correvon' (open bell-shaped, wine-red flowers; to 3m (10ft) tall); 'Purpurea Plena Elegans' (double, mauve-purple, pompon flowers; to 3m (10ft) tall); 'Duchess of Albany' (small, urn-shaped, deep pink flowers; to 2·4m (8ft) tall); 'Gravetye Beauty' (small, tulip-shaped, crimson-red flowers; to 2·4m (8ft) tall) and 'Bill MacKenzie' (open bell-shaped, yellow flowers with red anthers; to 7m (22ft) tall). See pages 20-2 for further cultivars and pruning details.

Clianthus puniceus **(lobster claw)** A semi-evergreen, scrambling shrub with arching stems, clothed with grey-green pinnate foliage, and striking red claw-shaped flowers in late spring and early summer. Grows to 3m (10ft). Recommended cultivars include *C. puniceus* 'Albus' with pure white flowers, and *C. puniceus* 'Roseus' with deep rose-pink blooms. See page 31 for pruning details.

Cobaea scandens (**cup and saucer plant**) A vigorous, evergreen climber, best treated as an annual (above). From summer to early autumn it bears large, bell-shaped flowers that open greenish-cream and age to purple. Grows to about 3m (10ft) in a season.

Cytisus battandieri (**pineapple broom**) A vigorous, deciduous shrub or small tree with soft, silvery-grey foliage and pineapple-scented, acid yellow flowers in mid-summer. Grows to 4m (12ft). Grow flat against the wall, cutting out old growth after flowering and training in the new.

Eccremocarpus scaber (**Chilean glory flower**) A fast-growing, short-lived perennial climber, best treated as a half-hardy annual (above). It bears attractive, finely divided foliage and showy, tubular, orange-red flowers from late spring to autumn. Grows to about 3m (10ft) in a season.

Ficus carica (**fig**) See page 68

Fremontodendron See pages 32 and 44

Humulus lupulus '**Aureus**' (**golden hop**) A vigorous twining perennial with rough stems and attractive golden foliage. Female plants bear yellowish clusters of bracts or 'hops'. Best in full sun but will tolerate partial shade. Grows to 5m (15ft), and is useful for training up trellis or growing into a large shrub or small tree. Cut back to ground level in early spring.

Ipomoea lobata (**syn. *Mina lobata***) A frost-tender perennial climber, best treated as a half-hardy annual (above). It produces three-lobed leaves and curved, tubular, crimson flowers, that fade to orange and then cream from summer to autumn. *I. tricolor* 'Heavenly Blue', has funnel-shaped, sky-blue flowers with a white throat, and lives up to its common name of morning glory because its blooms close in the afternoon. Both species grow to about 3m (10ft) in a season.

Itea ilicifolia A frost-hardy, evergreen shrub with holly-like, glossy, dark green foliage and greenish-white flowers borne on long catkin-like racemes from mid-summer to early autumn. It will grow to about 3m (10ft) when trained informally against a wall. Cut back after flowering to young sideshoots.

Jasminum (**jasmine**) A genus of shrubs and climbers grown for their usually scented, star-shaped flowers. *J. humile* 'Revolutum' is a semi-evergreen, stout shrub with pinnate, bright green foliage and fragrant, bright yellow flowers in summer; *J. mesnyi* is a slender-stemmed shrub with semi-double, yellow blooms in spring and summer. Both can be pruned after flowering, cutting back to strong growth lower down. On mature plants cut out one-quarter of the oldest stems at ground level. *J. officinale* is a twining, deciduous climber with fragrant, white flowers from summer to early autumn; and *J. polyanthum* is a half-hardy twining evergreen climber with strongly scented, white flowers, pointed in bud, from late spring to early summer. Both can be thinned after flowering to remove overcrowded growth.

Lathyrus odoratus (**sweet pea**) See page 60. *L. latifolius*, or everlasting pea, is a herbaceous, perennial climber with pinkish-purple flowers from summer to early autumn; 'White Bride' bears pure white blooms. Grows to 1·8m (6ft) or more. Cut back to ground level in late winter.

Magnolia grandiflora (**bull bay**) A frost-hardy evergreen tree with glossy foliage and large, fragrant, cup-shaped, creamy-white flowers from summer to autumn. 'Exmouth' is particularly hardy; 'Goliath' has very large flowers. Will attain 7·6m (25ft) and more, depending on the height of the wall against which it is growing. After flowering prune flowered shoots to within two to four buds of the framework.

Malus domestica (**apple**) See page 75.

Maurandya barclayana A half-hardy herbaceous perennial climber, best treated as an annual, producing trumpet-shaped, purplish-pink flowers from summer to autumn. Grows to 3m (10ft).

Mitraria coccinea See page 44

Mutisia decurrens A frost-hardy suckering climber with daisy-like, bright orange flowers in summer. Grows to 3m (10ft). *M. oligodon* has pink flowerheads from summer to autumn, and only grows to 1·5m (5ft). Does best with its roots in moist shade and its top growth in sun. Also protect from winter wet and cold, drying winds. Prune very lightly once new growth is obvious in spring, only removing dead or weak stems.

Parthenocissus quinquefolia (**Virginia creeper**) A vigorous deciduous climber, clinging by means of disc-like, suckering pads. Its dark green leaves are made up of five-toothed leaflets which assume brilliant orange and red autumn tints. *P. tricuspidata*, or Boston ivy, has three-lobed leaves and similarly striking autumn foliage: 'Veitchii' has smaller leaves which are purple when young and 'Lowii' has small, curiously crimped foliage. Both species grow to 15m (50ft) or more. In early winter trim to fit available space and remove from gutters and windows.

Passiflora caerulea (**passion flower**) A very vigorous, frost-hardy, semi-evergreen climber with unusual white and purple-blue flowers from summer to autumn, followed by egg-shaped orange fruit. 'Constance Elliott' has white flowers. Grows to 10m (30ft). In early spring shorten the sideshoots to within three to four buds of the framework.

Prunus armeniaca (**apricot**) A fairly vigorous self-fertile tree, coming into blossom very early in spring. In Britain, apricots do best with the protection of a sunny wall, and in good years will crop well from July to August. However they can be fussy trees and are prone to die back. Recommended cultivars include 'Alfred', 'Farmingdale' and 'Moorpark'. Apricots require a wall at least 2·4m (8ft) high.

Prunus domestica (**plums and gages**) A range of decorative and productive trees for both warm and cold climates, fruiting from August to September. They flower early in spring, therefore growing them as fan-trained wall specimens helps protect against frost damage. Although the following cultivars

are self-fertile (i.e. they do not need to be cross-pollinated), most will be more prolific if more than one plum or gage is planted nearby. For yellow fruit choose 'Oullins Gage' or 'Early Transport Gage'; for purple-blue fruit try 'Opal' or 'Marjorie's Seedling'.

Prunus persica (**peaches and nectarines**) A fairly vigorous self-fertile tree flowering in very early spring. If grown outside, they do best planted on a warm sunny wall and will produce fruit from July to September. All cultivars are susceptible to the disease peach leaf curl. Recommended peach cultivars include 'Duke of York', 'Peregrine' and 'Rochester', while 'Lord Napier' is a reliable nectarine cultivar.

Pyrus communis (**pear**) See page 76

Rhodochiton atrosanguineus A slender-stemmed, frost-tender climber, best treated as an annual. It has heart-shaped foliage and pendent, tubular, purple-black flowers protruding from lantern-shaped, pinkish-purple calyces from summer to autumn. Grows to about 2·4m (8ft) in a season.

Ribes speciosum An upright, deciduous, spiny shrub of borderline hardiness with fuchsia-like, dark red flowers in spring, and round, bristly red fruit. Grows to 1·8m (6ft). Best grown flat against a wall, cutting back flowered shoots to within two to four buds of the framework in late summer.

Roses – climbers and ramblers Indispensable, mostly deciduous groups of plants, providing summer colour and fragrance, and occasionally autumn hips. Roses do best on fertile, humus-rich, well-drained soil, which is fed and mulched on an annual basis. A small selection from the numerous cultivars available include: 'Albéric Barbier' (fully double, creamy white flowers; to 5m (15ft) tall); 'Aloha' (fully double, rose-pink flowers; to 3m (10ft) tall); 'Altissimo' (cupped, single, bright red flowers; to 3m (10ft) tall); 'Bobbie James' (large clusters of semi-double, creamy white flowers; to 10m (30ft) tall; useful for growing into a large host tree); 'Compassion' (apricot-pink flowers; to 3m (10ft) tall); 'Climbing Lady Hillingdon' (semi-double, apricot-yellow flowers; to 5m (15ft) tall); 'Climbing Iceberg' (double, white flowers; to 3m (10ft) tall); 'Dublin Bay' (double, bright crimson flowers; to 2·2m (7ft) tall); 'Félicité Perpétue' (fully double, pale pink to white flowers; to 5m (15ft) tall); 'Golden Showers' (double, yellow flowers; to 3m (10ft) tall); 'Madame Grégoire Staechelin' (fully double, clear pink flowers, followed by round red hips; to 6m (20ft) tall; useful for growing into an established tree); 'New Dawn' (double, pearl-pink flowers; to 3m (10ft) tall; tolerates partial shade). 'Wedding Day' (large clusters of single, fruit-scented, creamy white flowers that age to pale pink; to 8 m (25 ft) tall; useful for growing into a large tree). See page 39 for further cultivars and pruning details.

Solanum crispum **'Glasnevin'** See page 45

Solanum jasminoides **'Album'** See page 45

Sollya heterophylla See page 45

Trachelospermum jasminoides A frost-hardy, twining, evergreen climber with glossy, dark green leaves and fragrant, jasmine-like, pure white flowers from mid- to late summer. Grows to 3 m (10 ft). Prune in early spring if necessary to contain vigorous growth.

Tropaeolum majus **(nasturtium)** A vigorous annual climber with rounded leaves and red, orange or yellow flowers with a prominent 'tail'. *T. peregrinum*, or canary creeper, is another annual and has five-lobed foliage and fringed, bright yellow flowers. *T. tuberosum* is a frost-tender perennial climber with tubular, orange-scarlet blooms; it is wise to dig up and overwinter a few of its tubers in a frost-free place. All flower from summer to autumn, and grow to about 3 m (10 ft) in a season.

Vitis **(vine)** Woody, deciduous climbers with handsome foliage and often edible fruits. Three of the best ornamental cultivars with unpalatable purple-black grapes include *V.* 'Brant', whose green leaves turn bronze-red between the veins in autumn; *V. vinifera* 'Purpurea', whose purple and grey foliage turns rich purple at the end of the season; and the vigorous *V. coignetiae*, which has large heart-shaped foliage that turns bright red. The first two grow to about 7 m (22 ft), while the latter can reach 15 m (50 ft). See pages 24 and 69 for pruning details.

Wisteria Woody, twining, deciduous climbers with attractive, pinnate foliage and long racemes of fragrant, pea-like flowers in early summer. *W. floribunda* (Japanese wisteria) has the longest racemes of all, growing up to 90–120 cm (3–4 ft) long: 'Alba' has white flowers; 'Macrobotrys' has lavender-blue blooms. *W. sinensis* (Chinese wisteria) has lilac-blue flowers on 30-cm (12-in) long racemes. See pages 29 and 38 for pruning details.

Wall shrubs and climbers that will tolerate partial shade

Aconitum hemsleyanum **(syn. *A. volubile*)** A perennial, twining climber with three- to five-lobed leaves and hooded, purple flowers from mid-summer to early autumn. All parts of the plant are poisonous. Grows to 1·8–3 m (6–10 ft). Cut down to ground level in late winter.

Akebia quinata **(chocolate vine)** A semi-evergreen, twining climber with attractive foliage of five rounded leaflets, tinged purple in winter. In early spring scented, purple-brown flowers appear, then sausage-shaped violet fruits follow in autumn. Grows to 6 m (20 ft). After flowering, shorten growth by about a half to keep within bounds.

Ampelopsis glandulosa **var.** *brevipedunculata* A vigorous deciduous climber with vine-like foliage and insignificant flowers, sometimes followed by attractive round fruit, which are pinkish-purple at first then ripen to clear blue. Grows to 5 m (15 ft), and is useful for growing into an established tree. *A. glandulosa* var. *brevipedunculata* 'Elegans' is a slow, compact grower whose green foliage is attractively mottled with pink and white. It is also less hardy, so is best grown against a warm, sheltered wall. In spring, trim to fit the available space.

Berberidopsis corallina **(coral plant)** A frost-hardy, scandent climber with spiny, evergreen leaves and drooping clusters of spherical, crimson flowers on long red stalks (above). Grows to 3 m (10 ft). Plant in neutral to acid soil in a partially shaded, sheltered site. It does not respond well to being cut back hard, therefore only prune if essential, trimming back to fit the available space in spring.

Chaenomeles (Japanese quince) See page 28

Euonymus fortunei **'Silver Queen'** A bushy, evergreen shrub with leathery, white-margined, dark green foliage. Grows to 6 m (20 ft) as a climber. Little pruning is required other than to trim back badly placed branches or shoots.

Garrya elliptica See page 32

Hedera See page 81

Holboellia coriacea A vigorous, frost-hardy evergreen climber with attractive, palmate foliage and fragrant pinkish flowers in spring. Grows to 6 m

(20ft) and is useful for growing up into a tree in mild climates. Little pruning is required other than to trim to fit the available space in spring.

Hydrangea anomala **subsp.** *petiolaris* **(climbing hydrangea)** A vigorous, deciduous, self-clinging climber with fresh green leaves that turn butter-yellow in autumn, and white lacecap flowers in summer. Self-clinging evergreen species include *H. seemannii*, which is more tender and has large, narrow, leathery foliage, and *H. serratifolia*, which is similar but has broader leaves. All will attain at least 6m (20ft). After flowering, trim to fit available space.

Jasminum nudiflorum **(winter jasmine)** See pages 29 and 42

Lapageria rosea **(Chilean bellflower)** See page 44

Lonicera periclymenum **(common honeysuckle)** A vigorous, deciduous, twining climber with whorls of very fragrant, soft yellow, red-flushed flowers in summer, followed by sticky red berries. 'Belgica' flowers earlier than the species from May to June, while 'Serotina' blooms from July to September; 'Graham Thomas' has large, creamy-yellow flowers. *L. × americana* has large whorls of fragrant yellow flowers that are flushed with red from summer to early autumn. *L. japonica* 'Halliana' is even more vigorous and starts flowering in spring, producing less showy, pure white blooms that age to yellow. They all grow to at least 7m (22ft), and are useful for covering trellis or growing up into a tree. *L. × brownii* 'Dropmore Scarlet' is a semi-evergreen, twining climber with blue-green leaves and whorls of long trumpet-shaped, scarlet flowers in summer. *L. × tellmanniana* is deciduous, with bright copper-orange blooms from late spring to mid-summer. Both grow to 4–5m (12–15ft). *L. tragophylla* grows slightly larger, with orange-yellow flowers from mid- to late summer, followed by red berries. It also tolerates deeper shade than other honeysuckles. Prune them all back to strong young growth immediately after flowering.

Pileostegia viburnoides A frost-hardy, self-clinging evergreen climber with slim, leathery leaves and fluffy, creamy white flowerheads in late summer and autumn (above). Grows to at least 5m (15ft). Trim in early spring to fit available space.

Prunus cerasus **(acid cherry)** See page 82

Pyracantha (firethorn) See page 29

Schizophragma integrifolium A deciduous climber with clinging aerial roots and creamy white lace-cap flowerheads in mid-summer; *S. hydrangeoides* 'Roseum' is similar but has sharply toothed leaves and pink-flushed bracts. Both will reach 12m (40ft), and are most effective against a high wall, or better still allowed to grow into a large tree. Trim to fit the available space in spring.

Stauntonia hexaphylla See page 45

Tropaeolum speciosum A frost-hardy perennial climber with attractive palmate foliage and long-spurred, scarlet flowers from summer to autumn, followed by rounded, blue fruit. Grow in neutral to acid soil, with the roots in cool shade. It looks particularly good when grown against an evergreen backcloth of yew or box. Cut back to ground level in spring.

Gazetteer

Addresses

Barrington Court
near Ilminster, Somerset TA19 0NQ

Blickling Hall
Blickling, Norwich, Norfolk NR11 6NF

Cotehele
St Dominick, nr Saltash, Cornwall PL12 6TA

Erddig
near Wrexham, Clwyd LL13 0YT

Felbrigg Hall
Norwich, Norfolk NR11 8PR

Nymans
Handcross, nr Haywards Heath, West Sussex
RH17 6EB

Penrhyn Castle
Bangor, Gwynedd LL57 4HN

Powis Castle
Welshpool, Powys SY12 8RF

Sizergh Castle
near Kendal, Cumbria LA8 8AE

Westbury Court Garden
Westbury-on-Severn, Gloucestershire GL14 1PD

Additional National Trust gardens noted for wall shrubs and climbing plants

Acorn Bank Garden
Temple Sowerby, near Penrith, Cumbria
CA10 1SP

Bateman's
Burwash, Etchingham, East Sussex TN19 7DS

Coleton Fishacre
Coleton, Kingswear, Dartmouth, Devon
TQ6 0EQ

Castle Drogo
Drewsteignton, near Exeter, Devon EX6 6PB

Gunby Hall
Gunby, near Spilsby, Lincolnshire PE23 5SS

Hidcote Manor Garden
Hidcote Bartrim, near Chipping Campden,
Gloucestershire GL55 6LR

Knightshayes Court
Bolham, Tiverton, Devon EX16 7RQ

Lanhydrock
Bodmin, Cornwall PL30 5AD

Mottisfont Abbey Garden
Mottisfont, near Romsey, Hampshire SO51 0LP

Mount Stewart
Newtownards, Co. Down, Northern Ireland
BT22 2AD

Peckover House
North Brink, Wisbech, Cambridgeshire PE13 1JR

Polesden Lacey
near Dorking, Surrey RH5 6BD

Rowallane Garden
Saintfield, Ballynahinch, Co. Down,
Northern Ireland BT24 7LH

Sissinghurst Castle Garden
Sissinghurst, near Cranbrook, Kent TN17 2AB

Tintinhull House Garden
Tintinhull, near Yeovil, Somerset BA22 9PZ

Trengwainton Garden
near Penzance, Cornwall TR20 8RZ

Upton House
Banbury, Warwickshire OX15 6HT

Wakehurst Place
Ardingly, Haywards Heath, West Sussex
RH17 6TN

Wallington
Cambo, Morpeth, Northumberland NE61 4AR

Gardening books from the National Trust

In the same series:

Pots and Containers: A Practical Guide
Ever wondered how the gardeners at Ickworth achieve
that Mediterranean look despite the cold Suffolk winters,
or revelled in the exotic atmosphere at Overbecks in Devon?
Sue Spielberg talks to ten Head Gardeners and discovers
how they create these stunning effects in National Trust
gardens using pots and containers. Packed with tips from
the professionals with advice on when to take cuttings,
recipes for your hanging baskets, and hints on planting up
containers, this is a practical guide for the enthusiast and
the beginner alike.

More Practical Guides for 1999:

Gardening with Herbs
Gardening with Bulbs

More hints and tips from the professionals that you can't
afford to miss; Cathy Buchanan talks to the Head Gardeners
about their horticultural experiences with bulbs and herbs.

Gardens of the National Trust – Stephen Lacey
The ultimate armchair gardener's guide to the National
Trust's gardens from Acorn Bank, Cumbria, to the
Winkworth Arboretum in Surrey; from the re-created
seventeenth-century knot garden at Moseley Old Hall in
Staffordshire to the Arts and Crafts garden at Sissinghurst
Castle in Kent. Compare the formality of Hanbury Hall in
Hereford and Worcester with the quirkiness of Biddulph
Grange, Staffordshire, and the sheer exuberance of
Nymans in Sussex through the lavish illustrations that
accompany the text.

Gardening Tips from the National Trust
Seasonal hints and tips from National Trust gardeners –
from mulching to wildflower meadows, from pruning to
citrus fruit in pots.

The National Trust Gardens Handbook
A brief guide to 126 National Trust gardens with advice
on when to visit to catch their specialities at their best.

About the National Trust

The National Trust is Europe's leading conservation charity, looking after over 673,000 acres (272,000 ha) of countryside, 570 miles of coastline, 263 historic houses and 233 gardens and parks in England, Wales and Northern Ireland. The Trust always requires funds to meet its responsibility of maintaining all these properties for the benefit of the nation. To find out how you can help, please contact: The National Trust, 36 Queen Anne's Gate, London SW1H 9AS (0171 222 9251).

Membership
Joining the National Trust will give you free entry to properties and directly funds the Trust's work. For details of how to join, contact: The National Trust Membership Department, PO Box 39, Bromley, Kent BR1 1NH (0181 315 1111).

Legacies
Please consider leaving the Trust a legacy in your will. All legacies to the National Trust are used either for capital expenditure at existing properties or for the purchase or endowment of new property – not for administration. For more information contact: The Head of Legacies Unit, 36 Queen Anne's Gate, London SW1H 9AS (0171 222 9251).

The Royal Oak Foundation
This US not-for-profit membership organisation supports the National Trust's activities in areas of special interest to Americans. For membership and programme information in the US contact: The Royal Oak Foundation, 285 West Broadway, New York, NY 10013 USA (00 1 212 966 6565).

Index